DROPSHIPPING FOR BEGINNERS

The Ultimate Guide to Create a Dropshipping E-Commerce Business to Make Money Online from Home with Complete Marketing Strategies.

Jim Work

© **Copyright 2019 - All rights reserved.**

The content contained within this book may not be reproduced, duplicated or transmitted without direct written permission from the author or the publisher.
Under no circumstances will any blame or legal responsibility be held against the publisher, or author, for any damages, reparation, or monetary loss due to the information contained within this book. Either directly or indirectly.

Legal Notice:
This book is copyright protected. This book is only for personal use. You cannot amend, distribute, sell, use, quote or paraphrase any part, or the content within this book, without the consent of the author or publisher.

Disclaimer Notice:
Please note the information contained within this document is for educational and entertainment purposes only. All effort has been executed to present accurate, up to date, and reliable, complete information. No warranties of any kind are declared or implied. Readers acknowledge that the author is not engaging in the rendering of legal, financial, medical or professional advice. The content within this book has been derived from various sources. Please consult a licensed professional before attempting any techniques outlined in this book.

By reading this document, the reader agrees that under no circumstances is the author responsible for any losses, direct or indirect, which are incurred as a result of the use of the information contained within this document, including, but not limited to errors, omissions, or inaccuracies.

© **Copyright 2019 - All rights reserved.**

The content contained within this book may not be reproduced, duplicated or transmitted without direct written permission from the author or the publisher.
Under no circumstances will any blame or legal responsibility be held against the publisher, or author, for any damages, reparation, or monetary loss due to the information contained within this book. Either directly or indirectly.

Legal Notice:
This book is copyright protected. This book is only for personal use. You cannot amend, distribute, sell, use, quote or paraphrase any part, or the content within this book, without the consent of the author or publisher.

Disclaimer Notice:
Please note the information contained within this document is for educational and entertainment purposes only. All effort has been executed to present accurate, up to date, and reliable, complete information. No warranties of any kind are declared or implied. Readers acknowledge that the author is not engaging in the rendering of legal, financial, medical or professional advice. The content within this book has been derived from various sources. Please consult a licensed professional before attempting any techniques outlined in this book.

By reading this document, the reader agrees that under no circumstances is the author responsible for any losses, direct or indirect, which are incurred as a result of the use of the information contained within this document, including, but not limited to errors, omissions, or inaccuracies.

Table of Contents

Introduction ___ 9

Chapter 1: Understanding Dropshipping ___ 12
    What Is Dropshipping? ___ 13
    Who Is Dropshipping for? ___ 13
    How Does Dropshipping Work? ___ 14
    Why Should I Start Dropshipping? ___ 16
    Chapter Summary ___ 16

Chapter 2: Benefits and Disadvantages ___ 17
    The Benefits of Launching a Dropshipping Company ___ 18
    The Disadvantages of Launching a Dropshipping Company ___ 21
    Chapter Summary ___ 24

Chapter 3: Before Starting a Business ___ 26
    What Creates a Successful Business? ___ 27
    Leveraging Your Mindset for Success ___ 28
    Financially Preparing for Your Dropshipping Business ___ 31
    Chapter Summary ___ 32

Chapter 4: What's Essential ___ 33
    A Strong Platform to Launch With ___ 33
    A Clear Business Plan ___ 38
    A Commitment to Your Business ___ 43

Chapter 5: Dropshipping Stakeholders ___ 44
    Who Are Your Stakeholders? ___ 45

Chapter Summary _____ 48

Chapter 6: Positioning _____ 49

    What Does It Mean to Position Your Company? _____ 50

    Finding the Best Niche to Sell To _____ 51

    Tools to Help You Find Consumer Trends _____ 53

    Building Your Brand for Your Niche _____ 55

    Chapter Summary _____ 59

Chapter 7: Finding Best Selling Products _____ 60

    Niching Down On Products _____ 61

    Identifying the Best Products for Sale _____ 62

    Measuring the Competition _____ 67

    Chapter Summary _____ 67

Chapter 8: How to Find and Work with Manufacturers and Suppliers _____ 69

    Finding the Best Quality Suppliers _____ 70

    Qualifying Your Suppliers _____ 71

    Chapter Summary _____ 74

Chapter 9: Sales Channels and Marketing Strategies _____ 76

    Sales Channels for You to Use _____ 77

    Building and Operating a Sales Funnel _____ 80

    Chapter Summary _____ 83

Chapter 10: All about Orders _____ 85

    Security _____ 85

    Fraud Issues _____ 86

    Product Returns _____ 87

    Shipping Issues _____ 88

    International Shipments _____ 88

Dealing with Out of Stock Orders 89
Inventory 89
Chapter Summary 90
Chapter 11: How to Expand Your Dropshipping Business 91
Creating A "Rinse and Repeat" Approach 91
Reinvesting into Your Own Business 92
Chapter Summary 93
Chapter 12: How to Avoid Beginner's Mistakes 94
Worrying About Shipping Costs 94
Excessive Reliance on Vendors 95
Not Creating a Strong Customer Experience 95
Mishandling Order Issues 95
Not Creating a Return Feature 96
Chapter 13: Additional Tips 97
Have a Backup Plan 97
Invest in Your Marketing Skills 98
Automate Your Business Wherever Possible 98
Create a High-quality Website 98
Be Ready to Pivot When Needed 99
Chapter 14: Case History from Successful Dropshippers 100
Conclusion 103

Introduction

People have been making money on the internet since the internet was released to the public, and since then, we have found countless ways that the internet can be used to make money. From marketing and blogging to making videos and selling products to customers, there have been countless business structures introduced to the online marketplace since it went public around two decades ago.

These days, making money online from home is an important skill to have if you want to safeguard yourself against inflation and the increasing costs of living. By creating an online business that you run from home, you can effectively increase your monthly income without having to do quite so much to actually get that income into your bank account. When you create this passive income stream and build it into a large consistent income channel, you will feel confident that you have created a strong foundation for financial independence and freedom. As a result, you will no longer have to worry about finances in your life as you have successfully protected yourself and your family from financial worries.

When it comes to starting an online business to earn money from home, many people are looking for the best option to add to their existing careers. Since it is not feasible to quit your job and stay at home until your business earns enough money to be sustainable, chances are you are looking for something that is not going to require too much of your time to get started with. Moreover, you may also want to have a low startup cost involved with your online marketing business, so that you can save more of your money for important month-to-month expenses until your business begins to earn you a higher income.

If this sounds like what you are looking for, then dropshipping is an excellent online marketing business for you to consider. Dropshipping is a business model that allows you to run a complete retail business online without ever having to worry about managing the products in any way at all. Since products tend to be the most costly part of the business, both in terms of finances and time, it could help eliminate the need to directly deal with products in your business. When you begin your dropshipping business, all you need to do is create a channel for people to purchase through, find your suppliers, and market your products. The suppliers that you work with will be responsible for producing, storing, and managing order fulfillment with your products. This cuts out a massive portion of the work and financial investments that would otherwise fall on your shoulders in an online marketing business involving products, making this an excellent low-cost investment for people who want to earn money online.

These days, dropshipping has earned people anywhere from an extra $10,000 a year to an extra $5 million a year, and more. When it comes to dropshipping, there is truly no cap to how much you can make with your business, as long as you are willing to put the effort in to create and to grow your business and then to continually scale your business as you go. If you can identify how to grow your business and how to continually scale your business over time, you will have an easy time turning your dropshipping business into one that is earning your tens of thousands or hundreds of thousands of dollars, or even more.

In this book, that is just what we are going to teach you. If you are ready to begin discovering how dropshipping works, why it is worth getting involved in, and what you can do to make your dropshipping company a success story, it's time to begin. As you read through this book, I encourage you to take the time to really understand what each strategy is and why it works, so that you can leverage it to make the most success in your company. The more you understand the intimate details of a dropshipping company, the more you will be able to replicate this achievement with your own company and earn massive amounts of income from online marketing.

So, let's begin!

Chapter 1: Understanding Dropshipping

Before you begin any business venture, it is always a good idea to know exactly what you are getting into. This way, you can make an informed choice with your time and money. Furthermore, knowing what you are getting into means that you can have an easier time actually creating your business because you know exactly what it takes to create success with that business model, which means you are more likely to be successful overall.

Instead of jumping straight into talking about how you can find products and suppliers and how to build your dropshipping business, we are going to start with the very basics. Even if you have already learned about dropshipping in the past, I encourage you to read through the next couple of chapters with fresh eyes. Imagine that you have never heard of dropshipping before and that you are brand new to this concept, and that you are curious about how you can legitimately turn this into a business. This way, you are able to ensure that you have a strong understanding of exactly what it is that you are about to begin creating!

What Is Dropshipping?

To make it simple: dropshipping is a form of retail fulfillment where you have a company that is not responsible for keeping the products that it sells in its own possession. Rather than you being responsible for sourcing, purchasing, storing, shipping, and otherwise managing the products involved in your business, someone else takes care of all of this. When you sell merchandise from your store, the company responsible for your products will receive notification of the sale and fulfill the shipping for that product. They will also manage any returns or other product-related functions that need to happen in order for your business to run. You will only be responsible for paying that company for the products that you sell to your customers.

The possession of inventory and the way that inventory is managed are the primary differences between dropshipping and standard retail companies. If you were running a standard retail company online, you would be required to purchase, store, and manage your entire inventory. This part of running a retail business can be incredibly time-consuming, as well as expensive, which is why many people do not begin retail businesses. If you can cut this part out, however, you can make the business far more sustainable while still having the capacity to earn a fairly strong income from your business. This is where dropshipping comes in, and is why dropshipping can be such a powerful way to create an income with your business.

Who Is Dropshipping for?

Dropshipping is an excellent business model for just about anyone to get started with. If you are brand new to online business, if you are an entrepreneur looking to spread out your income channels, if you are looking to get into entrepreneurship but have a low budget, or if you are testing out a niche, dropshipping is excellent for you to get started with. This business model does not require a large amount of capital to start with, and it can offer a high payoff fairly quickly. If you remain consistent in your efforts and follow a proven successful strategy from the start, you can use dropshipping to help you earn more money while also learning more about the market.

I want to elaborate for a moment on the value that dropshipping has for helping you increase your market awareness and understanding. When it comes to getting involved in online marketing, it is important to understand the niche you will be selling and recognize how it works. Dropshipping can be a powerful tool for this because it could help you learn about a niche or a specific industry without having to invest too much capital into doing it. If you want to get started with online marketing in the health and wellness industry, for example, using dropshipping can assist you in identifying which niche will be the most accessible and profitable niche for you to get involved in. Then, once you have learned through dropshipping, you can either apply that knowledge to scale your dropshipping business or to launch alternative businesses in that industry.

When it comes to launching any form of business, it is essential to have adequate knowledge of that industry you are in and what it requires to generate success in that industry is important. If you take your time and use your dropshipping business properly, this can be a strong tool for helping you generate your own hands-on, proven analytics to teach you which part of your industry is most likely to be a success and how you can make it even more successful. So, whether you are a beginner or someone looking to spread out into other profit streams, dropshipping is an excellent choice for you to grow an online business.

How Does Dropshipping Work?

You already know that dropshipping works by you not having to be hands-on with your company's products in any way, shape, or form. When it comes to dropshipping, you are only responsible for marketing products and offering a place for those products to be sold on. To help you have an even stronger understanding of what this looks like and how it works, however, I want to outline the dropshipping process in a step-by-step method for you so that you are clear on exactly what needs to happen for this business model.

The first step in launching a dropshipping business is choosing your industry, building your brand, and creating a platform for your brand to existing on. You can do this by identifying and selecting any major platform that works for selling products online or by creating your own with a web developer. Once you have created your platform, you need to select products that will be for sale on that platform. Then, you need to create a sales funnel that will lead people to that platform so that they can see your products and purchase them from you.

After everything has been properly set up for your business, you need to begin the process of actually marketing your business. For this part, you are going to begin by marketing to your niche audience according to your sales funnel. In most cases, the first step is marketing on social media so that you can build brand awareness and help drive attention and traffic to your platform. Your primary focus will be on marketing the elements of your sales funnels properly, so in this way, you effectively reach the eyes of your target audience.

If your sales funnel is designed properly, all you will need to do is a market and create customer outreach. Then, your customers will find you and begin the process of moving through your sales funnel. If it is set up properly, you should not have to do much work beyond this as your customers will find you, land on your website, and then make a purchase.

Once the purchase has been made, a sale will be processed through your company platform. That sale will then alert your dropshipping supplier that a sale has been made, which triggers them to begin the process of packaging and shipping the product as per their company standards. They will also require a payment from you for each product that you sell, as this covers their costs of producing, storing, and shipping the products that you are selling.

When the product reaches the hands of your customer, the sale is then complete. At this point, unless they request a return or are otherwise unhappy with their product, the process is done.

Why Should I Start Dropshipping?

As you are about to learn in Chapter 2, there are countless benefits to launch a dropshipping business that supplies many reasons for why you should get started. The biggest reason, nevertheless, would revolve around finances. Dropshipping is one of the least expensive and most passive income streams that you can start using online. If you are someone who wants to increase your income but someone who does not have a significant amount of money to invest in something to help you with this, dropshipping is excellent. Not only it is going to help you earn more, but it is also going to do so in a way that is perfectly manageable, no matter how much or how little time you have to invest in it.

Due to the way that technology has advanced over the years, you can use countless automation tools to make dropshipping even easier. Through this, you can successfully design and promote your dropshipping company in the smallest amount of time possible. If you want to scale your business, the increased time that it will take to do so will still be minimal compared to other online marketing opportunities. For that reason, dropshipping is possibly the easiest and most lucrative business model for you to launch on the internet to date.

Chapter Summary

Dropshipping is an online retail business model where the individual who launches the business is seldom ever responsible for actually managing the inventory related to the business. Retail store owners never have to purchase, store, or ship inventory to customers in order for sales to be completed, as these tasks are instead done by a separate company, such as the manufacturer. Dropshipping is an excellent industry to get into if you are looking to supplement your income, test a niche market, or develop experience in a certain industry in the marketplace.

Chapter 2: Benefits and Disadvantages

As promised, we are going to discuss the benefits and disadvantages of launching a dropshipping company. Knowing exactly what you can expect, both in terms of the good and the bad, is important when you are interested in launching a new business. Staying realistic and knowing exactly what is expected of you and what you can expect from your business, is important in carving a path for success in your new business. The more realistic you are, the more likely you will be able to witness any possible risks or threats that may be lingering in the crosshairs of your business. Then, you can minimize these risks or divert these threats so that your business can continue to successfully grow and evolve over time.

As you read through this list, it is a good idea to consider how each benefit and disadvantage may impact you directly, too. Since you are singlehandedly going to be running this business, you need to think about how dropshipping's benefits and disadvantages will affect you if you get involved with this business model. This way, you can honestly assess whether or not this business model is going to work for you.

The Benefits of Launching a Dropshipping Company

First, let's address the benefits of starting a dropshipping company. As promised, there are several high-value benefits that you stand to gain, from launching a dropshipping company as a part of your efforts, to earn income from the internet. Below there are eight of the benefits that you will gain access to right away and as your company begins to earn greater income and offer you a higher profit over time.

Little Startup Investment

The first benefit is one that we have already largely discussed: there is very little startup investment when it comes to getting started with dropshipping. Considering that you are not required to purchase any inventory, store any stock, or otherwise manage products, you are able to launch your dropshipping company for a fraction of the cost of other possible business models. These days, there are also countless companies available to make your dropshipping company easier to run while also making it, even more cost-effective. This means that you can make it as inexpensive as possible for you to get started, which makes launching your business easier than it might be in any other marketplace.

Easy to Get Started

Not only it is a low investment to get started, but it is also easy to get started in general. Launching a dropshipping business ultimately only requires you to research a niche, build a brand for it, organize your platform, and then plug in suppliers' products. Once everything is put in place, all you have to do is continue to market your business and send people through the sales funnel that you have made for your company. Although it does take some effort to learn how to market properly and drive customers through a sales funnel, it is worth it, and it will create a large amount of success for your business in the long run. At the end of the day, learning to market is a lot easier than learning to market, purchase products, store products, ship products, and differently deal with products in your business.

Low Overhead Costs

In addition to having low startup costs, dropshipping also has low overhead costs when it comes to keeping the business running long term. The lack of involvement you have with the inventory means that you do not have to purchase stock, store the stock, ship the stock, or manage inventory differently to run your business. The most successful dropshipping companies are currently running from a home office for less than $100 per month. This will increase if you choose to scale your business larger, but even then, it will be significantly lower increases and costs compared to other retail stores or online marketing opportunities.

Flexible Location

Because of the fact that you are running your dropshipping business from your own laptop, you have the opportunity to be extremely flexible in how you run your business and where you run your business from. For example, you can run your business from your home office and continue to go on with your life as normal, if you desire. Or, if you want something more flexible, you can take your laptop with you and run your dropshipping company from virtually anywhere in the world. Again, since you do not have any involvement with inventory, you do not have to worry about relocating your business because all of your inventory will continue to be managed, as per usual, regardless of where you are in the world.

Access to Wide Selection of Products

If you were to launch a retail store where you would be responsible for managing the inventory, you would not have the opportunity to diversify your products without investing significantly more capital into your business. With dropshipping, you can diversify your products simply by choosing to add more products to your storefront. Essentially, any product available for purchase through the drop shipping manufacturer that you are using will be available for your company to sell online.

The one exception to this rule is if you choose to use a company like Amazon FBA, in which case you will have to purchase products and ship them to your inventory management company to manage the dropshipping part of the business. If you choose to run your business this way, you still have access to a massive variety of products, and you can diversify quickly so long as you follow the success strategies outlined in this very book in Chapter 9.

Easy to Scale

Since your only task in dropshipping is to market your products and nurture your sales funnel, this is an incredibly easy business model to scale with. You can effortlessly scale your business simply by adding more products to your storefront and increasing your marketing efforts to maximize your reach, and drive even more people through your sales funnel. As you will learn about in this book, scaling your dropshipping business can be nearly effortless. Furthermore, it can be automated to ensure that you are creating a strong growth strategy without using up too much more of your own time to do so.

Access to Global Market

In addition to having a diverse product lineup, you also give yourself access to a global market. Dropshipping is a business that is run online and, just like any other online business, you have the perk of being able to market your business in any country at any time. This means that you can effortlessly tap into a global market and maximize your sales rapidly, so that you can grow your business and have maximum reach. In the matter of running a business, the largest audience that you can target, the more likely you will be successful with your targeting.

Easy to Automate

Due to the nature of dropshipping, this particular business model is incredibly easy to automate. As long as you create a strong sales funnel, you can easily automate your marketing materials so that they post on their own throughout the month. With your marketing automated, all you have to do is to create the materials and upload them into an automation program for them to be released. In addition to automating the marketing part of your business, you can also automate the sales process through a simple POS (point of sale) system on your website. This way, everything is done automatically, and you do not have to work more than a couple of hours a week or a few hours per month to keep your dropshipping business running.

The Disadvantages of Launching a Dropshipping Company

As with any business model, dropshipping does have its setbacks. Not everyone will be successful with dropshipping, largely in part because they are not educated on what it takes to succeed, nor are they educated on the possible risks and threats. By educating yourself properly and clearly understanding what possible setbacks or risks you might face in your business, you can prepare yourself for anything and inevitably set yourself up for success. In this section, we will discuss the biggest disadvantages of dropshipping so that you are informed on what they are and how they can be handled to minimize their impact on you and your business.

Low-Profit Margins

Because of the fact that you have such minimal involvement in your business, dropshipping is known to have low profit margins. Unlike other businesses where you may be able to earn on your own a large markup, with dropshipping, you will have much smaller margins. You will need to factor in various expenses, including what it costs to run your website, marketing efforts, and to pay the manufacturers and suppliers who are creating and managing your inventory for you. After you pay all of these different stakeholders, you are going to find yourself with not a lot of profit at the end of each sale. For that reason, dropshipping is a business that needs high volume sales to ensure that you earn a decent profit from your company. Creating a sales funnel and marketing strategy that is prepared to handle high volumes of orders is the best way to ensure that you are prepared to create enough sales to earn a strong income from your business.

Inventory Issues

With a traditional retail store, you are responsible for stocking all of your own items and keeping your items in stock. You are also responsible for shipping those items and overseeing other things such as quality control. Although this does take more effort and expense on your end, it also means that you can guarantee everything from the amount of inventory you have to the quality of that inventory and the timeliness that it takes to reach your customer. In the matter of dropshipping, you do not have any involvement with the inventory, which means that the inventory issues could happen, and you are unable to do anything about them. These inventory issues can include having your inventory going out of stock without any warning, or they can arrive with questionable quality. If you are stocking inventory from multiple sources, this could get even more complex as you are now acquiring your products from even more sources. Mitigating risks and threats to your business from an inventory-related front comes from learning about how you can find the best suppliers, which we will discuss in Chapter 8, and how to manage your inventory as a dropshipper, which we will discuss in Chapter 10.

Shipping Complexities

Just like you can run into problems with inventory, as a dropshipper, you can also run into problems with shipping. Ideally, dealing with the shipping should not be an issue since the suppliers or the third-party shipping company, which you are working with, should be solely responsible for shipping. However, there is the issue that if the company has an issue with shipping, it is *your* reputation on the line, not theirs. This means that if you are not working with the best possible companies, you may end up having to apologize for a lot of shipping complexities.

Another complexity that many dropshipping companies run into is how much to charge for shipping. When it comes to shipping, you pay the supplier to ship your products to the customer. If you are sourcing products from multiple suppliers to diversify your inventory, you will find that each supplier may have different shipping costs. At this point, determining how much to charge for shipping can be a challenge since the costs vary so drastically from one company to the next. As well, if your shipping costs are not reasonable, then people are not going to buy from your business. The best way to deal with shipping is to decide what standard shipping costs you can charge that is reasonable and that will not cut into your own bottom line too much. This way, you might lose money on some sales, but at least your shipping will be consistent.

Supplier Errors

Just like you have to take the blame for inventory and shipping errors, you are also going to have to take the blame for any virtual errors that your supplier makes. Consequently, any error ranging from the products not being identical to the ones ordered to the products being low-quality or inconsistent, or anything else, is all going to come down on your reputation. If there are any items missing from shipping, or if shipping takes longer than expected, or if anything else causes problems in your supply line, you are going to have to take the blame for it. Unfortunately, even the best suppliers make mistakes, so you are inevitably going to have to take the blame and manage these mistakes to the best of your ability. Being polite, apologizing, and putting in the work to correct the error will all be your responsibility. The amount that you have to do this can be minimized by using higher quality suppliers and avoiding low-quality suppliers that are known for low-quality packaging and consistently poor fulfillment.

Overcrowded Market

Dropshipping is not a new business model, which means that there are many people in the industry trying to make a go of it so that they can begin to earn an income from the internet. This has led to a fairly saturated market with many people on each social media platform trying to sell for their dropshipping business. The disadvantage here is that you will have to fight harder to set yourself apart from the people who are already out there, trying to make an income through dropshipping. The positive aspect is that many of these people are using low-quality strategies to try and make a quick buck, meaning that it should not be incredibly hard for you to set yourself apart from these people. With the right marketing strategies and positioning efforts, you can make a much better impact on the market and earn far more money for your business than anyone else is.

Reliance on Suppliers

When you launch your own traditional retail business, you are responsible for bringing inventory in and then marketing it. Again, this involvement with inventory means that you can guarantee everything from product availability to quality and timeliness when it comes to the product reaching people who have purchased it. When you are running a dropshipping business, you rely on suppliers to uphold their best standards so that you can earn your best income. This reliance can be a disadvantage as it does mean that if the suppliers make any mistakes, you are on the line for them. It can also lead to huge issues in your business if you are not careful, as you may find yourself struggling to create a reliable and high-quality store until you locate the right suppliers. The key to offsetting this disadvantage knows how to qualify suppliers, so you can guarantee that they are most likely to offer your customers the best possible products, and experiences, with your business.

Basic Technical Skills

Although dropshipping is easy and requires very little effort, there is a certain amount of technical skills you will need to have to launch your business. The amount of skills that you will require ultimately depends on the strategy that you choose to use for getting your business out there. If you rely more on tools like Amazon FBA, Shopify, or anything else, you will not have to worry so much about technical tools as many of these platforms are fairly straightforward. However, you will still require a certain level of technical skills to help you get your products listed and on the market, and then in front of your audience. Fortunately, most of these technical skills will be explained to you right here in this book and, if they aren't, you can always watch a YouTube video to help you learn those skills as there are countless tutorials online teaching basic tech skills to beginners.

Chapter Summary

Creating a dropshipping business comes with advantages and disadvantages, just like any other business model. With dropshipping, your biggest advantage is that you have a low startup cost combined with low time investment requirements. You can easily launch a dropshipping business with $100-$250 and just a few hours on your hands. If you set it up properly, you can earn a significant income from your dropshipping business, too. Convenience and ease make dropshipping ideal for virtually anyone who is looking to start a business without wanting to put too much time into the process of actually launching, running, or scaling their business.

The convenience of the business does come with a price tag, however. When it comes to dropshipping, there are a few disadvantages that you need to be aware of. For example, you are not directly responsible for many elements of your business, such as inventory management, shipping, and quality control, yet you will be held responsible for these elements of your business. This means that your reputation may be out of your hands and at risk if you work with suppliers who are inconsistent or who are known for providing low-quality service to people. If you are not careful, you might find yourself taking a huge hit or even watching your business sink because of a failure to work together with suppliers who are actually going to provide high-quality service. Beyond that, you also need to be aware of the fact that dropshipping does have low-profit margins, so you are going to need to be prepared to sell a high volume of products in order to make a decent income through this strategy. By creating a high-quality sales funnel and using a strong marketing strategy, you will be able to drive a large amount of traffic through your sales funnel, hopefully increasing the number of sales that you make and drastically improving your bottom line.

Chapter 3: Before Starting a Business

Before you begin a business, it is always important to make sure that you are truly prepared to launch that business. Even with a business-like dropshipping, which does not require as much effort as other businesses, there is still a certain mindset that you must obtain to ensure your success? If you are not in the right mindset and don't have the right approach to your business, no matter how easy it is, you can almost certainly guarantee that you will fail in that business venture.

In this chapter, we will explore what it takes to set up a successful business, how you can get the right mindset for obtaining a success in your dropshipping business, and what you can physically and financially do to prepare for your business. This way, before you get started, you can guarantee that you are in the right frame of mind to succeed and to generate a significant profit through your business.

What Creates a Successful Business?

If you want to be successful in business, you need to be realistic, prepared, and willing. You need to be realistic about what you are going to face and what it is going to take, so that you are well aware of what needs to happen in order for you to generate a positive result in your business. You need to be prepared, so that you always have a plan for how you will proceed with things in your business, even if those things happen unexpectedly. Besides, you need to be willing to always work forward and find a way to guarantee a positive result for your business.

As an entrepreneur on any level, you are solely responsible for your success in business. No one will be as committed to your success as you are, so if you are not committed enough to make it works and see things through, the only thing that you can guarantee is your failure. You need to be ready to practically overcome anything that you face in business and in your life relating to your business. This means that if you are facing challenges regarding how to manage the finances of your business, you have to be prepared and willing to overcome that problem. If you are facing challenges with your own motivation and consistency with showing up and marketing your business, you need to be prepared and willing to overcome that problem. No matter what you face in your business or life that impacts your business, you need to be prepared and willing to exceed those challenges so that you can get success in your business.

When asked, virtually every entrepreneur will tell you that their success comes from one thing: their mindset. Through having the right mindset, they have been able to identify solutions to problems that seemed impossible to defeat. With the right mindset, entrepreneurs have moved mountains to make their businesses successful, and they have had the energy to remain committed to seeing it through even when it seemed unlikely. As a result, they were able to guarantee their success by guaranteeing that they would not give up until they were successful. That is exactly what you need to be ready to do if you are going to start a successful dropshipping business, or any business, online or anywhere else in this world.

Leveraging Your Mindset for Success

Since your mindset is the most important aspect of your business, you should be prepared to learn how to leverage your mindset for achieving a success. Many people who launch a dropshipping business are new to the industry, therefore they are new to the requirements that it takes to make a successful run in the industry. It is not uncommon for dropshippers to be individuals who are just starting out, who want to earn a side income, or who are looking to use dropshipping as a tool to teach them about the industry in general. In all of these scenarios, the mindset that is required to be successful may seem foreign and unknown. To help you get started, we will discuss the five most important mindsets that you need to have in place to help you generate achievement in your dropshipping business.

Be Fearless

Starting anything new in life can be terrifying, especially if you have high stakes involved in the new venture that you have chosen to begin in your life. If you want to be successful in business, you will have to develop the mindset of being fearless to help you overcome any possible challenges or setbacks that you may face along the way. In business, there are countless hurdles that you are going to have to face, but the biggest one that people tend to underestimate is the fear of actually getting started. Many people put so much pressure on what it means to get into a business that they find themselves consistently backing out before they even begin, which will prevent your business from growing in obvious ways.

To develop a mindset of fearlessness, you do not actually have to *be* fearless. Instead, you simply need to behave like you are fearless. This means that you "feel the fear and do it anyway," as they say in the business. In other words, even if you are afraid and you think something is going to be challenging or possibly impossible, you take the time to actually go ahead and give it a try anyway. The worst that can happen is: you fail to make the results that you had hoped you would make, and so instead, you must use this failed attempt as a lesson to apply toward future efforts.

Develop Your Leadership Qualities

Even if you are the only "employee" that you have in your business, developing your leadership qualities is crucial to running a successful business in any industry. Teaching yourself how to become a better leader by improving your skills that directly affect your leadership means that you will have an easier time leading yourself, and anyone else that may come into play in your business. Developing your fearlessness qualities is a great start, but there is plenty more that you can do to help you grow your leadership qualities to become an even better entrepreneur.

Leadership qualities are not only going to help you direct people in your business, but they will also help you motivate others and inspire them to join your venture, effectively helping you grow your business. Through leadership qualities, you will have an easier time acquiring customers, partners, stakeholders, and investors who are interested in supporting you in your venture. Without these qualities, you might struggle to really sell your vision and get yourself out of there, which can massively hold your business back.

Always Look for Solutions

When it comes to business, you can guarantee that you are going to face several challenges. If you look at any successful business that is well-known in its industry, you can guarantee that throughout its history, it has faced major challenges in reaching that level of success. Even companies like Amazon and Coca-Cola have some noteworthy "failures" in their histories that come from facing challenges that they ultimately had no obvious solutions for. Even though the solutions they chose may seem like failures to their consumers, to the company, these solutions became major learning strategies that educated them on how they could become their best.

As an entrepreneur, the only way you will get through any challenge in your business is through being willing to look for the solutions to the challenges that you are facing. This means that if you had a launch that fell flat, you need to be ready to find a solution. If you have a supplier that is not pulling their weight, you need to be willing to look for a solution. If you have customers that are consistently unhappy with a certain element of your business, you need to be willing to look for a solution. No matter what problem you are facing, you always need to be willing to look for a solution so that you can provide your business, and your customers, with the best quality services possible.

Be a Grateful Person

Gratitude is a huge tool when it comes to growing your business. These days, many have earned the reputation of being entitled or ungrateful by failing to show their gratitude for their business and everyone involved in making their business a success. Virtually every industry is far more diverse than it once was, which means that the companies who behave this way rapidly lose business as people go elsewhere to companies that genuinely show gratitude for their business. If you want to achieve in your own business, you have to develop an attitude of gratitude and openly show it to the people who are partaking in your business.

When you run your business, always show gratitude for everyone. This means that even the suppliers who are helping you run your business should frequently be shown gratitude as it makes them more likely to offer you and your customers the best services possible. You should also be showing gratitude to your customers and everyone else in your business and even your entire industry. The more you can show gratitude to people, both openly toward the public and privately behind closed doors, the better your reputation will be. People will see you as being a business that is pleasant to work with, making it more likely for them to actually want to do business with you. As a result, you will be far more likely to grow and earn money with your business.

Surround Yourself with Inspiration

There will be many personal challenges that you face when it comes to handling a business, even if that business is not going to consume much of your time, like dropshipping. Every entrepreneur who has ever generated success in their businesses, regardless of whether or not the business was part-time or a full-time gig, have faced their own personal challenges that have made handling a business difficult for them. If you want to be successful in running your own business, you need to be ready to overcome the personal challenges that you face, which make handling a business more difficult.

Surrounding yourself with inspiration is a great opportunity to help you exceed these challenges, as inspiration can remind you that there is a strong reason for why you are moving forward with your business. The more you surround yourself with inspiration, the more you will be lifted up and supported every time you need it. This means that you will have a much easier time generating success and scaling your business over time. Do not be afraid to join groups, follow inspirational people, and network with those who inspire you. The more you can surround yourself, the better you will do in the long run.

Financially Preparing for Your Dropshipping Business

On a practical level, before you launch your business, you will need to financially prepare for your dropshipping business. The average investor or financial advisor will tell you that you should be prepared to financially carry your business for 3-6 months with funds out of your own pocket, to ensure that you are able to manage the finances of your business until it becomes profitable. Others will tell you that you need to be prepared to financially carry your business for 9-12 months, as this is a more likely timeframe for your business to generate enough profit to break even consistently.

On the issue of dropshipping, your startup costs and overheads are often quite low, so it is unlikely that you will need to save too much to launch your business with. However, having that extra money already put aside means that you are not going to have to worry about the finances of your business, so that you can effectively keep your business up and running while you work out the marketing aspect of things and drive traffic to your website.

With dropshipping, a saving of anywhere from $500 to $5,000 is ideal to help keep your business afloat for at least 6 months while you develop your business. The exact amount that you will need will depend on what way you choose to use to get your business out there. One that is run through suppliers and a basic storefront will cost less, whereas one that is run through a company like Amazon FBA, where you have to purchase your own products and pay for storage and handling fees, will cost more.

Chapter Summary

Getting started with your own business requires a certain amount of mental and practical preparation to assist you in really generating the desired level of success in your business. If you want to be successful with dropshipping, you have to create the right mindset to help you lead your business to success. In other words, you need to learn how to become fearless, solution-oriented, driven, grateful, and inspired. You also need to be ready to learn how to continue nurturing and growing your mindset over time to really generate success with your business.

In addition to mentally preparing yourself, you also have to practically prepare for launching your dropshipping business. The best way to prepare yourself financially is to save enough money to allow you to run your business for six months without eating into your monthly income. This way, as you run your business, you can feel confident that you have the money available to keep you going until you begin to make sales. Taking this financial pressure off of yourself early on will prevent you from feeling desperate and pushy with your sales, making it easier for you to make your earliest sales. Then, those sales will generate enough momentum to grow your business and your bottom line, and keep you in the green going forward.

Chapter 4: What's Essential

Now that you are well aware of what it will take for you to get started with dropshipping, it is time for you to start to understand the practical aspects of starting, launching, and running a dropshipping business!

For the rest of this book, we will focus on a strategic step-by-step process that you can use to help you launch your dropshipping business. You should use these steps to ensure that you are taking the necessary steps to build a strong foundation and a strong system to maintain your dropshipping business with.

A Strong Platform to Launch With

The first thing you need to do is start with a strong dropshipping platform. When we refer to a strong dropshipping platform, what we are talking about is the sales channel you will use to get your products in front of your audience. For dropshipping, there are countless platforms that you can use to put your products in front of your audience, effectively reaching them so that you can earn sales. In Chapter 9 we will discuss all of these channels in-depth so that you know how you can get your products in front of the right people.

Using these platforms is not just about sales, though, it is about managing your entire business. Regarding managing your dropshipping business, you will need to have one key platform that you use to manage your entire business online. This platform is going to be your main "hub" for where you do business from. Here, you will track your inventory, make sure that your other channels are functioning properly, upload new products, manage your marketing strategies, supervise customer service inquiries, and otherwise conduct your dropshipping business.

There are six eCommerce platforms that you can consider using as your main channel or main platform for your dropshipping business. They include WooCommerce, Magento, BigCommerce, OpenCart, Shopify, and Amazon FBA. Below, we will talk about all six of these channels in greater depth so that you can confidently pick the right channel for your needs.

WooCommerce

WooCommerce is the most popular tool to use for eCommerce in general, including for dropshipping retail businesses. This tool is not only the most popular, but it also has the most market share over any other eCommerce platform across the globe, holding more than 28% in the overall eCommerce industry. This is large because WooCommerce is an easy plugin that you can upload into just about any platform for free, and it allows you to manage your entire business, complete with inventory management and a point of the sales platform for you to use.

WooCommerce has one of the easiest graphic user interfaces out there, making it easy for even beginners to use. It also has a huge community of designers and developers who use it on a consistent basis who can help you navigate the system as needed. Beyond that, millions of stores online are hosted by WooCommerce, so you know that it is functional, reliable, and capable of creating a strong foundation for you and your dropshipping business online. WooCommerce is even used by larger companies like Ripley's Believe It or Not, Weber Grills, and Singer.

Magento

Magento is the second-largest eCommerce platform across the globe, and it has just as much power and flexibility as WooCommerce. That being said, it is not nearly as user-friendly and tends to be far too complex for new users to really get the swing of. Unless you already have a strong tech background, you might find that Magento is too challenging for you to understand and use in your business. Magento does have a huge support system, however, so if you are confident in your knowledge and want to give this system a go, you will have access to a lot of people who can assist you with navigating Magento's errors and troubleshooting the system as needed.

Like WooCommerce, Magento is completely free and can be plugged into nearly any platform, making it easily accessible for people who want to minimize their expenses online. Magento hosts hundreds of thousands of eCommerce stores, including top brands like Dufry, JCB, and Selco BW.

BigCommerce

BigCommerce is known as a "hosted eCommerce platform" meaning that the software does not function as a plugin, but instead allows you to host your entire website on their platform. BigCommerce hosts more than 50,000 small businesses and 2,000 enterprise companies, with well-known brands like Toyota, Nine Line Apparel, and Marucci Sports using the platform.

This platform is easy to use, features a free trial period, and can be easily customized to suit your requirements and your branding. Packages range from $25 to $250 per month depending on the size of your business, with enterprise packages having undisclosed prices that are discussed upon calling in and chatting with a representative. To get support in using your BigCommerce platform, you simply call, email, or chat into their customer care line to receive support.

OpenCart

OpenCart is a free platform that can be set up in a matter of minutes, as long as you have a basic understanding of tech and internet set up. This platform offers free and paid versions, with a free plugin or paid to host features that you can use for your business. Naturally, the paid features will be more efficient and attractive and will offer the best user experience for anyone looking to grow their business on OpenCart.

OpenCart is fairly straightforward to use, with most of their features being a point and click style; however, you will have to customize which features you are using, which can take some effort on your behalf. You will have to decide what plugins you want and how you will organize them to create a platform that practically supports your business, while also hosting a strong customer experience on your platform. The support with OpenCart is fairly easy with ticket and email style support systems that you can use to discuss your concerns with developers. You can also use the community support forums to gain assistance from other people who are using OpenCart, which is often plenty to solve any issues you may run into with the platform. Recognizable websites that are hosted on OpenCart include for Fans by Fans, British Red Cross, and 6 Dollar Shirts.

Shopify

Shopify is a popular name in the eCommerce industry and is undoubtedly one of the most powerful platforms for dropshipping that there is. This platform offers a high-end plugin called "Oberlo" which helps you completely manage dropshipping businesses from the platform itself. With Oberlo, you can stock your store as well as manage fulfillment processes in a virtually painless manner, making your store a powerful tool that you can use to make money with. Even if you do not have a single tech-savvy bone in your body, and you have no idea how to run a business online, Shopify can make the process easy for you.

Shopify is extremely user-friendly, with an interface that is easy to navigate, and that helps you set your store up in just minutes. You can also use pre-filled pages that help you share information about your store, your privacy policy, your return policy, shipping information, and even a shipping calculator to help you easily set up your store on Shopify. The prices range from $29 to $299 per month with undisclosed enterprise pricing that you can opt for if you call in and discuss the packages with a representative.

Getting support from Shopify is as simple as plugging into their 24/7 email, chat, or phone support as needed. There is also a built-in forum where you can receive support for your business as needed. Beyond that, you are not going to find much help for Shopify as the platform is hosted as a proprietary business, meaning that no external open forums exist for users to gain support from other users. Some of the most noteworthy websites that are using Shopify for hosting include companies like Negative Underwear, Flatspot, UgMonk, and Pipcorn.

Amazon FBA

Amazon FBA operates differently from other platforms, as it does require you to purchase inventory and have it shipped to Amazon's warehouses for the shipping process to take place. That being said, if you do choose to run a dropshipping type business this way, Amazon has an incredible platform set up for you to run your business online. Amazon FBA is an exclusive, hosted platform where you gain access to your own storefront and your own hosting services with your membership.

For Amazon FBA, you pay $39 per month plus storage, shipping, and handling fees to manage your business. It is arguably more expensive than any other option, although it does offer a significantly higher profit margin if you learn how to run your business effectively. Through this platform, you can keep track of inventory and products and ensure that everything stays stocked for your business to keep running. Otherwise, Amazon handles your inventory storage and management, shipping and handling, customer returns and inquiries, and all customer service related inquiries that come in through your Amazon interface. While it is more expensive, it is also more passive and hands-off than any other dropshipping company out there; aside from having to order your own products and having to ship to Amazon.

A Clear Business Plan

To really generate success with any business, you need to have a business plan. A business plan is a guideline for how you will strategize, build, grow, and run your business. Before you launch your business, your business plan should be made as a guideline for you to follow, as it will feature information starting all the way back to the conception and official "launch" of your business. This will provide you with action steps before you ever even begin to announce your business to other people, ensuring that you take the right course of action every single step of the way.

Creating a clear business plan for your dropshipping business should be simple, clear, and focused on helping you reach your goals in your business. You could create a traditional business plan for your business which requires a significant amount of information and research to do, or you could create what dropshippers call a "lean startup format." This leaner format requires less time to complete and includes less information. For a business as simple as dropshipping, it can be far easier to work with over a traditional business plan which can take a lot of time, research, and effort to put together. In addition to being more convenient while still including all of the information that you require to launch your dropshipping business, your lean business plan is also easy to adapt as needed, so that you can keep your business plan updated. For a business as simple as dropshipping, this modality is far more ideal than anything else.

On the issue of creating a lean business plan for dropshipping, there are seven things you want to pay attention to that will help you create a strong and functional business plan. These seven things include your brand identity, problems and solutions, customers, competitors, channels, revenue streams, and expenses. Considering and preparing for these seven areas of your business will help you create the strongest business plan for your dropshipping company.

Below, we will briefly discuss how you can prepare each of these seven elements of your business plan for you to use as you launch your dropshipping business.

Identity

When you begin a business, you should always have a clear understanding of who you are and what you have to offer with your business. This begins with you identifying your business so that you are prepared to introduce your brand identity to the industry, and to your customers.

Before you can announce your identity to anyone else, you need to have a clear understanding of who your identity is for yourself. This way, you know exactly what and who you are introducing to other people, which makes it easier for you to introduce your brand with confidence and clarity. The best way to identify your brand for your lean startup business plan is through creating a paragraph or two that identifies what your shop is, who your audience is, and what products you plan on offering your customers. This should be plenty for you to get started with, as you will come to know your business more clearly as you continue to develop and market your business to others.

Problems and Solutions

Every single business is going to run into problems along the way, whether they want to or not. Problems are a common experience in business that can make running your business challenging, especially if you are not prepared to face those problems. This is one of the key reasons why having a business plan makes sense in the first place: because it helps you identify what problems you might face and what you can do about them.

To prepare your startup plan, make sure that you identify some problems that you are likely to face and what you are going to do about them. The problems that you need to consider are going to be specific to your industry and your unique circumstances, so for this part, you may need to do a quick internet search on what types of problems you may face and what solutions you are going to consider helping you overcome these problems.

As well as identifying likely problems, you can also identify general solutions that you are going to use in general situations. For example, you may not know exactly what problems you will face in marketing, but you can still identify a strategy for how you are going to overcome unexpected problems related to marketing. The same goes for customer acquisition and customer service, supplier-related issues, quality control issues, and any other issues that you may face with your dropshipping business. Again, a quick search on your unique industry and how it tends to behave in dropshipping is a great opportunity for you to discover what problems you need to be aware of and what solutions you need to consider to keep your business running.

Customers

A business is not a business without customers, which means you need to take the time to understand who your customers are and what it will take for them to buy from your business. You can build a section in your startup plan about your customers by taking the time to consider who they are, as well as any other information that you might need to help you market to them and increase your sales.

As you identify who your customers are, you want to put a significant amount of effort into discovering which demographic they are from specifically. Many businesses collect this information by creating a "customer profile" which is essentially a character sheet for your customer. With this, you create your ideal customer, or your exact target customer, like a profile on paper. This means that you identify who they are, where they live, how much money they make, what they like to spend their money on, and what type of marketing strategies most appeal to them. By identifying who your customers are and what they care about, you give yourself the best opportunity to make sure that you are effectively reaching your target audience in all of your marketing efforts.

Competitors

No matter what industry you are in, you are going to have competitors. Many new-age marketing guides falsely guide you to identify who the top performers are in your industry, which will actually take you away from the information that you need to succeed. Attempting to compete against massive corporations when you are just starting out makes no sense, so I strongly advise you not to take this approach to identify who your competitors are to aid you in your success. Instead, know who the top-performing corporations are in your industry so that you understand where to gain inspiration for marketing strategies and positioning.

Differently, consider your competition to be the people who are on the same level as you are in business. Thus, anyone who is just starting out and anyone who is in their first one or two years of business should be considered your competitors for the time being. Identify who else is just starting out or who else is just ahead of where you are at right now and keep your eyes on these businesses, as these are the businesses that are your direct competition.

After you have identified who your direct competition is, you want to keep down their information so that you can keep an eye on them. Your competition is going to help inspire you to identify where you can improve your business, what you can do to offer better services, and how you can make a better reach with your own audience. You can also learn from them in terms of what does not work and what needs to be adjusted in order for success to happen in any particular strategy or angle.

Channels

Businesses require different channels to reach their audiences and attract their audiences into their shop. Using these channels is crucial to help maximize the number of potential customers that you reach, so that you have the best chance at reaching people who are going to purchase from your audience. Remember, the more people who come through your sales funnel, the more people who have the potential to help put money into your pocket.

In your business startup plan, you should have a clear understanding of what channels you will be tapping into to help you create success in your business. Later in this book, we will go through several marketing channels that you can go through to help you create success in your dropshipping business. You will want to take note of each of the channels that you plan on using for your business so that you are clear on how you plan on reaching your customers to bring money into your dropshipping business.

Revenue Streams

When it comes to creating a dropshipping business, the way that you are going to make money seems fairly straightforward: you get people onto your website, and they purchase from you. Therefore, you will need to identify what revenue streams you are going to use to assist you to get in front of your audience and generate sales within your business.

The easiest way to fill out this part of your business plan is to identify what the dropshipping process looks like, or what your sales funnel looks like. This means that you want to identify where you are bringing customers in from and what process they are going through to land on your page, so that they can shop from your business. Ideally, this process should be fewer than three clicks until checkout to ensure that the process is simple and straightforward. The easier you make the purchasing process for your customers, the easier it will be to have them actually go through with it and purchase from you.

Expenses

Lastly, you want to identify what expenses you are going to have in your business. This includes any fees you will pay for paid marketing, for your website, and for any other fees that you are going to need to pay to keep your dropshipping business running. The best way to identify what your expenses are going to be and keep them organized and easy to find is to look through your sales funnels and identify which parts will require you to pay for a product or service. This way, you know that you are tracking all of your expenses that are going into running your business. You also know that you are not going to be adding in any unnecessary expenses as you go, due to not having a clear plan in what you need to invest in and what can wait until later.

A Commitment to Your Business

Aside from choosing your platform and creating a strong business plan, you also need to have a commitment to your business. Your commitment to your business is a great opportunity for you to make sure that you are staying focused on generating the best possible business that you can create. In the case of making a commitment to your business, there is one excellent way that you can do it that will also serve as a piece of marketing material. That is: creating a mission statement or a value statement.

Creating a mission statement or a value statement is your opportunity to identify your commitment to your business, while also being able to tell everyone else just how committed you are to make your business the best quality business possible. This statement is simple to make as it only requires one or two sentences about your commitment, including what it is that you are committing to the offering. For example, if you are committed to offering high-quality, trendy, simple, sleek, advanced, or modern products, you should outline this in your mission statement. If you are committed to offering the best service, or customer service, or unique service, this should be outlined in your mission statement. Anything that you are committed to offering within your business should be identified and shared with your audience. This way, you both know what you have committed to, and you can hold yourself and your brand accountable to meet these commitments through everything that you build within your business.

Chapter 5: Dropshipping Stakeholders

In business, stakeholders are the people who are going to be responsible for developing your business with you. In dropshipping, your stakeholders are not directly involved in investing in your business, nor are they going to be "partners" with you as you develop your business along the way. Instead, they are groups of people who are required for your business to succeed. That being said, your stakeholders can be anyone who you feel is the best fit for your business and who fits in best with what you are creating and offering.

In this chapter, we will discuss who your stakeholders are so that you know who is that you need to be working with to generate success in your business. Furthermore, it is important that you take care of each of your stakeholders to ensure that they will receive everything that they need to continue doing business with you. If you stop taking care of your stakeholders by respecting them and offering them what they need in order to continue doing business with you, you will find that your business rapidly falls apart and you lose all profits that you may have otherwise gained.

Who Are Your Stakeholders?

In dropshipping, you have three to four stakeholders who are important in your dropshipping process. You need to make sure that all three or four of these stakeholders are being taken care of your business so that you can stay up and running. These stakeholders include manufacturers, wholesalers, retailers, and consumers. You will likely engage with all four of these stakeholders unless you choose to go through wholesalers only, in which case you will not be doing business with manufacturers, and so you will not need to worry about them as you grow your business.

Below, we will discuss all four of these stakeholders, including how they contribute to your business and what you need to do to ensure that they are well taken care of. This way, you can keep your business running and generate great success through your strategy and planning.

Manufacturers

Manufacturers are the stakeholders who are directly responsible for creating the products that you are going to be selling. Most manufacturers do not sell directly to the public, so you may not work directly with manufacturers in your dropshipping business; however, they are a necessary part of your business's success as, without them, you would not have access to products to sell.

If you do find a manufacturer that you can buy directly from for your dropshipping business, you can expect to pay significantly lower prices, as these are the only suppliers on the market who have next to no markup on their products. Instead, they offer them at a cost that comes out to the cost of what it takes to make the items both in terms of physical product and labor. Working with a manufacturer will require you to purchase minimum quantities and then keep that stock somewhere for you to hold onto until it gets into the hands of your customers. For most dropshippers, they do not purchase directly from manufacturers unless they are using a platform like Amazon FBA, where they can store their products at the warehouse and continue to use the dropshipping structure for their business.

If you do work with manufacturers, you need to make sure that you are doing so with the maximum level of respect toward your manufacturers that you can have. The best way to show respect to your manufacturers is to understand what their procedures are for purchasing products from them and then following those procedures exactly. This means that you should be clear on what you need from them, get your order in on time, pay them in full on time always, and differently provide them with the information and resources that they need to create your products. By being consistent and considerate with your manufacturers, you can feel confident that they will enjoy doing business with your brand and that they will continue to do business with you as long as offering high-quality services the entire time.

Wholesalers

Wholesalers are the individuals who purchase from manufacturers, place a small markup on products, and then offer those products for sale to retailers. Wholesalers often offer lower purchase quantities than manufacturers do, as they purchase the larger quantity and then sell out to multiple smaller retailers. Working together with a wholesaler is the most likely way for dropshippers, as many wholesalers have organized their companies to be efficient for drop shipping needs.

Purchasing from wholesalers requires the same level of respect and consideration that you would give to a manufacturer. You need to inquire about what their purchasing procedures are and then ensure that you are always following these procedures in your business. Doing so ensures that everything runs smoothly and that they are given the best opportunity to ensure that your customers are satisfied. If you are not properly following the wholesaler's procedures, including how to order and how to pay for your orders, chances are your orders are not going to be fulfilled as effortlessly as possible. As a result, both you and your customers will pay the price with orders not being fulfilled in a timely manner. This will ultimately come down on you, as your reputation will be the one that is jeopardized along the way.

Retailers

In your dropshipping business, you are the retailer. The entire business entity that you are building is the retailer in this chain of stakeholders, and just like with any other stakeholder, you need to understand how this one works and what you can do to respect your business and yourself. In any business, the retailer is the company responsible for putting merchandise into the hands of the consumers. Their entire job is to create a storefront for their consumers to purchase through, so that customers can buy the products that went through the channels of the manufacturers, wholesalers, and retailers.

The best way to respect yourself and your retail shop in this chain is to make sure that you have clear, strong boundaries from the start. You need to have these with yourself and with anyone else who intends on doing business with your company. These boundaries should be designed to protect you from any individuals or companies who are offering low-quality attention or services to your brand. This means that if you have a consumer that is repeatedly scamming your business, you need to respect your business by blocking that person from being able to purchase any more stock from you. This also means that if you have a manufacturer or supplier who is causing problems for your business, you no longer engage in doing business with them.

At the end of the day, both of these strategies contribute to the ultimate way that you can respect your business which is through honoring, building, and maintaining a strong reputation for yourself. Anytime you engage with people, companies, or activities that are jeopardizing your success, you are directly working against your company and disrespecting your own efforts and the efforts of anyone else who may be involved with your business. Instead, do yourself a favor and protect your asset by doing all that you can to build and protect the reputation of your brand.

Consumers

Consumers are your customers, which is anyone who browses and shops from your store. Understand that when you are working with stakeholders, your customers are not just people who have actively purchased, but they are anyone who has even considered purchasing. After all, people who have considered purchasing but who have not yet purchased are people who are quite possibly going to become customers in the future.

For your business, customers are just as important as your manufacturers or wholesalers. Without either of these stakeholders, you would not have a business as you would have no one to buy or supply products for your business. You need to respect your customers just as much as you respect your manufacturers and wholesalers by ensuring that you do everything that you can do to give them the best possible experience with your business. This implies that you should have a strong brand that is enjoyable for them to do business with a great customer experience that makes working with you easy, and amazing customer service that is going to help your customers with any problems that they may experience.

Chapter Summary

When it comes to running any business, there are stakeholders who are involved in your business model. Stakeholders receive some form of money, service, or goods from your business and are necessary for the wellbeing of your business. For dropshipping, your stakeholders include manufacturers, wholesalers, retailers, and customers. Each of these stakeholders requires a certain treatment in order to be respected as a necessary part of your business and to help keep your business afloat. You can support these stakeholders by ensuring that their needs are met and that you are pleasant to work with, as this is the best way to ensure that your business continues to operate harmoniously. Not respecting or looking after your stakeholders can result in the failure of your business, as each of these links is a crucial part of your success. If you do not continue to respect and maintain each link, you will find that you do not generate as much success because you have failed to maintain your roster of stakeholders. Before anything else, always consider each of your stakeholders and how your business moves will impact them, and what you can do to ensure that all moves you make in your business positively affect everyone involved.

Chapter 6: Positioning

Positioning your company is an essential way to get your brand on the market and reach the eyes of the right people in your industry. Every single brand is known for engaging in positioning their company in one way or another, as this is the only way that they can really begin to build a strong reputation for themselves. If you want to generate success in your business, you will need to identify the right position for your brand and then stand sternly behind that position.

As you create your position for your brand, it is important to understand that you can never fully guarantee your position. You are certainly capable of influencing and impacting where your brand is going to be positioned, but you cannot guarantee that you will receive the position you aim for. That being said, you can always continue to adapt and evolve your business until you reach that position. Alternatively, you might find that you reach the right position for you to maximize your profits, even if this position is not the exact position that you were aiming for.

In this chapter, we will discuss what a position is, how you can determine what position you want to have for your business, and what you can do to aim yourself for that position. This way, you can begin to set your company up for the strongest reputation and positioning right from day one.

What Does It Mean to Position Your Company?

Positioning your company in the market means that you are choosing where in your industry you will fall in relation to other businesses. Your position will impact your reputation in the industry by ultimately teaching people what to think about your business and how to think about your business. For example, if you position yourself amongst the higher quality brands in your industry and design your brand in a way that encourages people to compare you to them, you are likely going to build the reputation of being a higher-quality brand. Alternatively, if you position yourself amongst the brands that are known for offering the best deals or the most unique experiences, then this is the reputation that you will be aiming to create.

When you position, you are not only positioning your brand but you are also positioning your products or services. In other words, you have to teach your customers where your whole brand falls in the marketplace, as well as where each of your individual products and services falls in the marketplace.

If you are effective at positioning, your customers will see you and identify you as being the exact brand to meet their needs over anyone else. Your best positioning will come from having a unique selling proposition that you can offer your customers, which is unlike anyone else in your marketplace. In addition, it should be able to be measured in *relation* to other brands in your marketplace so that people can determine what they can expect from you before ever shopping with you.

Creating your position in relation to other brands means that you are building your reputation based on the reputations of other brands. So, for example, say you are offering makeup and beauty products for sale in your dropshipping business, and you want to be recognized as one of the highest quality shops on the market. You might consider positioning yourself amongst companies like Sephora, Mac Cosmetics, Yves St. Laurent, and other upscale makeup companies so that when people see your brand, they automatically assume that you are high-quality. In this way, you are leveraging other company's well-established brands and reputations to develop your own reputation, effectively positioning you amongst the best right from day one.

Of course, you are likely not going to be directly competing with companies this large, but this gives you a great understanding of what it is that you are trying to achieve with positioning. To summarize: you want to leverage other company's existing reputations to develop your own reputation right from the start, effectively helping you build your reputation even before anyone has actually done business with you.

Finding the Best Niche to Sell To

Positioning yourself with dropshipping first requires you to find the best niche to sell to. The niche that you pick is going to be the unique segment of your industry that you will position yourself in, so that you have specific people to market to. This way, when you begin marketing your business, you have an easier time reaching your audience. In the online marketplace, there is a common saying that goes: "if you speak to an audience that is too large, you speak to no one." In other words, if you do not get extremely specific in whom you are talking to; you are not going to be talking to anyone because no one will be listening.

Creating your specific audience to speak to starts with, knowing which niche will be the most productive for you to sell to. You need to pick a niche that will be relevant to the industry that you want to be in, while also being profitable enough for you to make money in that niche.

Finding a niche for your dropshipping business will take five steps, each of which we will discuss in greater detail below. Following these five steps will help you pick the exact audience that you need to target, so that you can sell directly to an audience who will be most likely to actually buy from you.

Step One: Pick Your Passion

The first thing you need to consider when you are finding a niche for you to sell to is what you are passionate about, or at least what you are interested in. Attempting to sell to an industry or a niche that you do not particularly care about, or have any interest in, is going to be challenging. To put it simply, you are not going to have the level of passion, understanding, and determination that it will take to create success in that particular niche. Instead of trying to get into a niche that makes no sense to you, get into a niche that will help you generate maximum levels of success in your business, by picking one that you like and that you already have a basic understanding of.

Step Two: Solve Some Problems

As with any business, you need to be able to solve your customer's problems so that you have a solution that you can sell them. Selling solutions is much easier than selling mere objects, so make sure that you identify what types of problems your customers have so that you know exactly what solutions they are in need of. Knowing what solutions you are selling will not only help you find your niche, but it will also help you pick your position in the marketplace.

Step Three: Find a Crushable Competition

While you qualify possible niches that you can be a part of, look for ones that have a competition that you can truly compete against. Trying to get into any industry that is saturated with high-quality solutions at prices that are better than you can offer is only going to result in you wasting your time. Rather than trying to force yourself into a market that has no room for you, look for one that is ready for your products and services and begin to position yourself in that space. This way, you already have a competitive edge, and you are ready to crush any competition that you may face with your business.

Step Four: Identify Profitability Factors

Next, you need to identify how profitable your niche is going to be. For some niches, no matter how great it might sound to you, there may be no one actually readily willing to spend money on your particular products. In this case, the niche is not profitable or not profitable enough, which means it is not worth your time to get involved in the niche in the first place. Rather than trying to force profits out of a low profiting niche, identify a niche that will have plenty of profitability for you to capitalize on right from the bat. This will make it far easier for you to gain the profits that you desire from your business.

Step Five: Test It Out

Lastly, you need to test your niche out. Nothing fares better than hands-on testing, which is exactly what you are going to need. You can test a niche out by preparing and planning a launch for a business and then marketing as if one is actually going to launch. If you have chosen a high-quality niche, it should be easy for you to market to your target audience and begin to generate pre-launch traffic with people who are interested in your business concept. If you have chosen a low-quality niche or one that is not going to help you generate much success, it will be challenging to gain interest early on which may inform you that the niche is not ideal for you to pursue. In this case, since you have not actually established a business in it or haven't begun selling anything, you can easily pivot to choose a niche that will be more successful for you to build into.

Tools to Help You Find Consumer Trends

Learning how to find and read consumer trends is crucial in helping you place yourself in your industry and continue to place yourself, as you evolve your business and offer more products in your lineup. When it comes to running a dropshipping business, you need to use consumer trends to help you identify which niche will be the strongest niche for you to build into. You also need to use these trends to help you discover which products you should offer to this niche, and which products you can add to your shop to help you continually stay in front of your ideal audience. The more you can stay on trend or, better yet, ahead of the trends, the more you will be seen as relevant and worth shopping with.

These days, there are plenty of tools that you can use to help you identify consumer trends so that you can position yourself perfectly and evolve seamlessly with your industry. You should use these tools right away to help validate your niche, ensuring that you have chosen the best position in the market for yourself and your brand. Once you have chosen that spot, simply keep an eye on these tools so that you can continue to keep your strong positioning.

Google Trends

Google Trends is a great tool that you can use to help you identify what industries and niches are trending in any given market. With this tool, you can access it for free and simply type in your industry or your niche and select your chosen market. You can choose a single country or a global market to help you identify whether or not your chosen industry is trending. This website is updated weekly, meaning that trend reports are fairly relevant and will give you a great idea as to whether or not your chosen industry is presently strong enough to handle another business in.

In addition to researching your industry, you can also research new products that you are considering launching in your store. Google Trends will help you determine whether or not these products are actually popular, and if they are worth selling or not. Beyond telling you information about that exact product, this tool will also let you know which alternative search terms are popular in that particular category, assisting you to find alternative products that you could consider selling as well.

Trend Watching

Trend Watching is another great trend watching tool that you can use to help you identify where consumer trends are going and how you can leverage these trends to grow your business. Trend Watching offers a free tool that you can use to identify market trends, allowing you to get in front of your target audience with the best trends possible. As well as helping you research a specific industry, Trend Watching features a large blog that offers great insight as to global trends and various trends taking place in each individual industry. These blog articles can be great resources to help you identify what measures you can take in your business to stay ahead of the curve with many new trends, while also trailblazing new trends in your industry. At the very least, following these trends can help you get a feel for where your own industry is going and what you can do to stay relevant with your audience.

Building Your Brand for Your Niche

The final step in positioning yourself is making sure that you have a brand that is actually going to get you into the right position with your business. Branding says a lot about a company, and not having the right brand in place can rapidly deteriorate the quality of your positioning strategy. If you want to position yourself effectively and be discovered by the right audience, you need to build an audience that is comparative to the brands that you want to recognize as your competitors.

For example, if you want to enter the market being seen as a brand that already offers refined, high-quality products, you need to create a brand that is comparative to brands that have already been operating in your niche for 3-5 years. This way, rather than being seen as a new brand that doesn't have a clue, you are seen as a more mature and refined brand that offers high-quality products and exceptional services right from day one.

Creating a strong brand takes many layers, and often it takes time to really refine your brand and create the best experience possible. That being said, you can launch your dropshipping business with a strong brand to start with using just four steps. These four steps include: identifying your image, creating your message, carving out your clique, and validating your brand with your audience. We are going to discuss each of these steps in further detail below so that you can create a brand that will put you as close to the position that you are aiming for right from day one.

Identifying Your Image

Every single brand has an image, just like every single person has a look. If you want to have a brand that looks refined and high-quality right from day one, you need to develop an image that you can consistently maintain throughout every single piece of marketing material that you create and share with your audience. This means that your graphics, font, colors, and general image all come together to create one single appearance that is identifiable by your audience.

When it comes to creating your image, the key is to create a diverse image that flows together seamlessly. You want to have consistency in everything without being overly repetitive or creating an image that appears unrefined or incomplete. This means that your graphics should all flow together, even if they do not feature the exact same subjects every single time. Likewise, your fonts should all flow well together, and so should your colors too.

You can create a strong brand image by creating a brand board using a platform like Pinterest. Brand boards are created by grouping together images, fonts, and colors that are all similar in appearance and style. The goal is to create a general theme that you are going to use as a guideline to create your brands' image with. Once you have stylized your brand with a branded board, you can use this as a tool to measure your marketing materials by. Ideally, marketing materials should all fit in together with your brand board as though they were meant to be a part of it all along. As long as each piece of marketing material fits into this general image, you can feel confident that they are all flowing together well to create a strong, consistent, recognizable brand.

Creating Your Message

Together with an image, or a look, you also need to have a message. Your message is what you are saying to your audience. You will use your brand message to help you identify your tone and the way that you speak to your audience. In this way, every time you speak to your audience, the way that you speak and the messages that you share are consistent, allowing you to always come across with the same purpose in every marketing piece that you share.

Creating your brand message is simple: identify what you want to say to your audience, and go with that. Ideally, your brand message should be as simplified as possible, as people are not going to wait around long enough to identify what your message is if you take too long to get it across. For example, rather than saying: "use this eco-friendly product to help you live your best life while also saving the ocean, so that you are no longer contributing to problems like pollution," your message should be "become a part of the solution with our eco-friendly products." Keeping your message refined and to-the-point means that it is easy for you to share, and it is easy for your audience to pick up on.

Once you design your primary message, you need to decide how you will share it with your audience. You can choose how you will share it by picking your tone and sticking with that tone throughout all of your marketing materials. It is important that, for the most part, all of your materials are designed with the same tone as this contributes to the consistency in your brand's personality. So, if you choose to create a happy and inspired tone, you need to consistently create happy and inspired pieces of written content to share with your audience. If you choose to go with thoughtful and educated, then everything that you write needs to be thoughtful and educated. Although you can share with a different tone from time to time, virtually everything you share should be consistent with your chosen tone.

Carving Out Your Clique

The final step in designing your brand is carving out your clique, or deciding who you want your brand to resonate with. By now, you should have already done some basic research on who your target demographic is for your business plan. In this case, your target audience should be who your clique is. Now, all you need to do is really get to know your target audience in a more concise way by spending some time with them online and getting to know how they behave and who they really are. At this point, you are taking your customer profile and identifying real people who you can get to know, allowing you to turn your customer profile into a real-life image of whom you are marketing to.

As you continue to hang out with your target audience online, get a feel for who they really are and how they really behave. Pay attention to the nuances that make them unique from any other person online, and identify what about them makes them the perfect customer for your audience. This way, when it comes time to building your clique online, you already know who they are, how you can reach them, and what it will take to make them a part of your customer base.

Validating Your Brand with Your Audience

The final step in building your brand image is validating your brand with your audience. Every single audience will have a preference in terms of what images they like the most, what colors they respond best to, and what tone or message style they resonate with. You want to make sure that you have cultivated a brand that will specifically speak to your audience and captivate them in a way that makes them actually interested in following you and purchasing from your brand.

You can validate your audience by paying attention to your competitors to see how they have built their brands and by comparing your brands to theirs. Notice any patterns that exist in their brands, such as certain styles they lean toward, colors they use, and messages they convey, and notice how your brand fits in with these patterns. A strong brand should fit in with these patterns *without* directly copying any other brand in its industry so that it comes across as unique yet relevant, and competitive.

To further validate your brand with your audience you can begin to build a branded profile and test to see how many people in your target audience actually pay attention to your brand. If your brand is well-designed, it should be easy for you to attract attention using the brand that you have put together. If not, you may need to adjust your brand to create a more suitable image for your customers, making it easier for them to fall in love with your brand and begin following your business and purchasing from it.

Chapter Summary

Your brand requires a strong position if it is going to make an impact in your chosen industry. Positioning is your only opportunity to control your perceived reputation, as it allows you to decide which brands you want to be directly compared to when people come across your brand in the industry. You can position your brand by identifying where you want to fall in the market and then choosing a niche that will help you land in that position. After you have chosen that niche, you need to validate it and then build a strong brand that is going to help you get into that particular position in the market. Branding is your biggest opportunity to design an image, personality, and reputation that defines whether or not you are worthy of being seen in the position that you desire your brand to be seen in. By creating a strong image and message for your brand, while also clearly defining who you want your brand to be attracting, you can create a strong platform for you to position with. Make sure that you validate your brand with your chosen audience to ensure that they are actually interested in your brand and willing to do business with you.

Chapter 7: Finding Best Selling Products

Now that you have carved out your place in the market, you need to start identifying what products you are going to sell in order to make money with your business. One of the biggest mistakes that dropshippers make is overstocking their shops with every single product that even remotely fits into their brand. Doing this is said to help increase the number of opportunities that you have to earn money from your business because now you have plenty of options for your customers to choose from. Instead, what ends up happening is that your customers become overwhelmed by the number of choices and instead find themselves looking elsewhere for the products that they were originally looking for. Furthermore, stocking too many items in your shop can result in your shop quality looking cheapened because you have more of a department store feel to you than a specialty shop. Naturally, shoppers want a specialty shop to purchase with as this provides an image that appears to be of higher quality and, therefore, more worthy of investing their cash into.

In this chapter, we will discuss how you can pick products that are going to sell in your business. The way that we are going to do this is by picking products that will be highly targeted toward your niche and most likely to sell. This way, rather than relying on one or two sales each of hundreds of different products to make sales, you are relying on a higher volume of sales through a fewer number of products. In the end, you will find that this builds your brand reputation and also improves your sales numbers, ultimately earning you a much greater income than any other strategy.

Niching Down On Products

In the previous chapter, you identified the best niche to build your brand in so that you can market toward an audience who is more likely to purchase from you. Now, we will use this chosen niche to help you find the best products that are most relevant to your niche, and that are the most likely to help you earn sales in your business. The products that you are going to select will directly contribute to your branding and the position that you build for yourself, so you want to make sure that you are choosing the best products for the job.

In what concerns selecting which types of products are going to be the best for your branding and positioning, there is one thing that you really need to focus on having within every single product. That is relevancy.

Every single product you choose to stock your store with should be relevant to what your niche actually is, in a highly specific manner. In other words, if it does not directly make sense to sell it in your niche, you should not be selling it at all. You do not want to begin selling products that are relevant to neighbor niches or to niches similar to yours, as this will end up confusing your audience as to what your niche actually is. For example, if your company sells sleek, modern yoga supplies, you should not also sell sleek, modern lunch boxes just because your customers also eat food, possibly right after yoga sessions. This may seem like it makes sense because then your consumer can purchase their yoga supplies and the lunch boxes that they would eat their food with after their session, but to your customer, it will just be confusing. Refrain from selling anything other than exactly what you said you would sell. This way, when people land on your page, they know exactly what you have to offer and they do not have to attempt to remember who you are or what you are selling them.

In addition to making it easier for you to carve out who your brand is and what you have to offer, keeping to your niche makes it easier for you to market and make sales with your products, too. At the end of the day, if you become known for one specific thing and you market exclusively to that niche, your customers will likely not even remember that you sell anything else. This means that if you try to branch out into other niches and you do not do it as a part of a strategized business move, chances are your audience will forget that you even have those products available. As a result, they probably will not come to your business to shop for those products, anyway, because they would not expect for you to be the brand carrying those products.

As you will learn about in Chapter 11, there are certain instances where you can branch out into neighboring niches and begin offering other products to your audience. This, however, should always be a highly calculated and strategized move that is used to grow your business and expand your sales in a logical manner. It should not be something that you attempt to do right away before your audience even has the opportunity to figure out who you are and what you have to offer them.

Identifying the Best Products for Sale

Now that you know how to qualify your products for your niche, you need to make sure that you pick the best products to sell in your business. Even with relevancy factored in, you are going to have to make sure that you are picking the right relevant products to earn an income with. In light of picking products for your dropshipping business, you need to make sure that you choose products that are popular, profitable, priced right, high-quality, and marketable. Below, we will discuss how you can qualify each product to make sure that it properly fits within these categories and serves your business in reaching your target sales numbers and income goals.

Picking Products That Are Popular

The first and possibly most obvious thing that you want to do for your business is picking products that will be popular amongst your niche audience. You want to make sure that you will be selling things that people actually want to be buying. Picking products that are popular will help you with creating a strong shop that is filled with interesting, attractive items that excite people and encourage them to pay attention to your shop.

You can identify which products are the most popular in your industry by going to platforms like Amazon and Etsy and searching for keywords that are relevant to your industry. Doing this will take you to the category relevant to your business, which will then show you the most popular items that people are purchasing. Depending on what platform you are on, you may need to adjust your sorting settings to say "Top-Rated" or "Best Selling." Choosing these search parameters will ensure that everything that is being shown to you is what people are actually purchasing on a regular basis, and not just what has been posted or sponsored by the people selling said product.

After you have searched on these platforms, you will get a general idea of what types of products are selling the best. Then, you can use platforms like Google Trends to do research on said product so that you can begin to see whether or not it is actually popular enough for you to stock in your shop. Ideally, the product should have a strong uptrend behind it, but it should not be at its peak trend. Any product that is in peak search numbers, based on the parameters given to you by platforms like Google Trend, is likely to be too competitive for you to make sales in. You want products that will be popular, but not oversaturated to avoid having to attempt to compete with far too many brands that are already out there selling products to your target audience.

To help get your shop started, you want to identify about 30-50 popular products that you could sell in your shop. This may sound like a lot, but it will be narrowed down through the following steps to about 15-30 new products that you can stock your shop with. This is plenty for a new dropshipping company to start with and leaves you with space for growth over time, so avoid going much higher than this number.

Pricing Your Products Effectively

As you go through the most popular products that you could potentially stock your shop with, you want to make sure that you also jot down how much money you could charge per item. This is going to be helpful with determining what your profit margins would be later on, while also giving you an idea of how you can use your price points to position yourself in the market.

When it comes to price points, you want to look around and see what the exact same products are going for in other shops. As you do, seek to identify the lowest price point in the market and the highest price point in the market. Then, try to identify the most popular price point, which will be the price point that has made the most sales. You might expect that the lowest price point would be the one making the most sales, but the truth is most consumers consider products that are priced too cheaply to be cheaply made. In many instances, dropshippers that are pricing at the lowest possible prices are seen as companies that work with low-quality suppliers, resulting in people being skeptical about ordering through their business at all. For your business, you want to price around the mid-point or slightly lower or higher, depending on what you want your positioning to be. If you want to be considered inexpensive or affordable, you want to make sure that you are using the lower end of the midway point. If you want people to perceive you as being a more high-end boutique shop, the price is recommendable to be slightly higher. This way, you leverage your pricing as your positioning as well by using it to help influence how others perceive your business.

Ensuring that the profit Margins Are Big Enough

After you have identified the ideal products that you can stock your shop with, you want to make sure that your profit margins are big enough. Your profit margins are calculated based on the amount of money that it is going to cost for you to stock items in your shop, versus the price that you are going to sell your products at. To calculate your true price points, you need to factor in the cost of running your business combined with the cost of the product itself when you order it from your supplier.

Ideally, the products you sell should have at least a 30% or larger profit margin as this will ensure that you produce enough money to pay for listing and selling the product, while also making a profit on top of that. Anything too far below 30% is going to likely prove unworthy of selling as it will not earn you enough to really run your business. Unless you are making a decent profit margin that covers the cost of selling that product and you are selling high volumes of it, there is no point stocking anything with a lower margin.

It is important to understand that the more popular your products are in the industry, the less your profit margin is going to be because you have such a large competition amongst you. This is why it pays to pick products that are popular but not overly saturated, as it helps ensure that you are getting the right profits and attention on your products for you to succeed with.

Finding High-quality Products to Sell

Next, you need to make sure that you are factoring in quality. Remember, even though there are multiple stakeholders involved in you earning money with your business, you are the one who is growing a reputation. If you have not focused on sourcing high-quality products from high-quality suppliers, you might find that your reputation takes a drastic hit and that it completely destroys your ability to make any money with dropshipping. It pays to take your time and find suppliers who will offer the highest quality of products and services to your audience so that you have the best opportunity to earn a strong reputation and, therefore, more sales.

We will discuss more how you can find and qualify suppliers in chapter 8, but know that this is crucial in helping you decide whether or not you should stock a product in your store. If you cannot find the best quality of product with a great supplier, it is better to refrain from stocking that product at all. Instead, continue looking until you find the right supplier, and in the meantime, stock your store with other products that your customers will enjoy.

Considering How Marketable a Product Is

Another thing that you need to consider how marketable a product really is. In light of stocking your store with anything, if you cannot see a clear way that you could market that product to your audience, it might not be ideal for you to stock that product at all. The products that you stock should make sense and should be easy to incorporate into your marketing strategy, especially because a large part of your marketing strategy comes from talking about and sharing the products that you are selling in your business. You should be able to easily identify how you could photograph the product, how you could incorporate that photograph into your marketing strategy, and what you could say about that product in order to maximize your sales. If you cannot clearly identify how all of this would fit together while still operating well within your brand image and personality, it may not be the best product for you to stock in your store.

Your Personal Experience

If you chose the right niche for you, you should have some interest in the niche already, meaning that you also have some level of personal experience with that niche, including products within that niche. In other words, you should be able to consult with yourself and ask simple questions like "would I be interested in a product like this?" or "would I truly spend money on something like this?" Ideally, you should only stock your store with products that you could truly see yourself purchasing or considering so that you feel confident that every product in your store is something that someone else would consider, too. When people land in your store, you want them to feel like they have plenty of great options, not like they are shopping for a single diamond in the rough. They should not have to hunt for the one interesting product in your whole shop, as your whole shop should be filled with products that they find interesting. This way, they actually stick around long enough to buy something!

Measuring the Competition

The last part in deciding which products you will stock your store with is to decide if you can truly measure up against the competition. Considering the competition was an important part of qualifying your products, but now you need to consider it more critically. The key here is to look at the competition and see what they are selling, and then determine whether or not you can actually step into the market and keep your competitive edge. Ideally, you should be able to clearly identify how you can stay competitive in the market by discovering what you have to offer that your competition is not already offering. Even if you find that you are offering the same products, determine how your pricing or branding can be leveraged to create a unique experience that bodes a strong competitive edge against your competition. This way, you can ensure that your products are more likely to be chosen over anyone else. Especially early on with a brand new business that has yet to establish a strong reputation, you will need to make sure that you have a competitive edge that gives people a clear reason to shop with you over anyone else.

Chapter Summary

Your products are a crucial part of your business as they provide your customers with something to purchase. Without your products, there is nowhere for money to come into your business because there is nothing for people to buy from you. Choosing the right products is crucial as this is your opportunity to make sure that you are creating a strong image for yourself, while also creating a strong opportunity for people to buy with you.

You want to make sure that your products are supporting your positioning by picking products that clearly fit in with your niche, while also picking products that you will be able to price effectively within your business. You want to leverage your price point as a part of your positioning strategy, too, so make sure that with your ideal price point you still have a strong profit margin. This way, you can leverage your products and prices to establish your positioning within the market while also still earning a strong income.

Always make sure that you have a strong competitive edge with your products to ensure that people choose to shop with you over anyone else. The more reasons you can give people to shop with you over other brands, the more likely people will choose you over anyone else. This way, you maximize your chances at success in your dropshipping business.

Chapter 8: How to Find and Work with Manufacturers and Suppliers

Manufacturers and suppliers are as crucial to your company as your customers are. If your business lacked manufacturers and suppliers entirely, it would fail to take off because you would have no products to sell to your customers. If your manufacturers and suppliers were low-quality or struggled to fulfill the demands of your business, your reputation would be tarnished due to their tardiness. Finding the right manufacturers and suppliers for your business is crucial if you are going to succeed, as they will provide you with products to sell and services to boost your business's reputation with.

In this chapter, we will discuss everything that you need to know about finding the best suppliers for your business. This way, you can feel confident that you will be growing your best business right from day one, allowing you to have a strong foundation to land on and grow from as you continue to develop your dropshipping business.

Finding the Best Quality Suppliers

Finding the best dropshipping suppliers requires you to know what you are looking for and to know where to look. When it comes to suppliers, it does take a specific skillset to find where they are and to qualify them to ensure that you are working with the best possible suppliers. Manufacturers, wholesalers, and other suppliers tend to be more challenging to find because they are not known for having a strong online presence. Unlike retailers, who need to leverage social media and other platforms to get in front of consumers, suppliers rarely develop any form of online presence because they do not need to. Instead, they are more hidden and do require some effort to find. This is because, in the past, you simply spoke with your network to find the best suppliers for your business, and your network of other business-oriented people would put you in touch with the suppliers that you needed. Before eCommerce grew into what it is today, the business was more exclusive, and it was harder for people to get into retail or any other form of business, so there was no need for suppliers to market on a mass scale.

In addition to looking on Google, there are other platforms that you can use to help you identify dropshipping companies that can stock your shop for you. Alibaba has been a well-known name in the dropshipping industry since its conception, with the platform being a great tool for people that are looking to connect with suppliers. Alibaba operates similar to Amazon or eBay with a search engine type platform that allows you to search for certain products and find the suppliers who make or sell the products. Shopify offers a great option, as well, with their plugin "Oberlo" which has already discovered and qualified suppliers, so all you need to do is plug the products into your website and go. Alternatively, you can use a directory like World Wide Brands to help you identify companies that are actively using the dropshipping model to get their supplies from their warehouses to consumers.

It is important that as you search for dropshipping suppliers, you look for suppliers who are going to actually be able to fulfill the dropshipping service. If they are not, you will need to either search for other suppliers or consider using a third party company like Amazon FBA to complete the dropshipping portion of your business.

To get started with qualifying and finding the right suppliers, you should compile a list of approximately 5 suppliers that you could go through to help you stock your shop. This list will likely go down to 1-3 suppliers in the end which will ultimately become the suppliers that you are going to work with when it comes to actually stock your dropshipping storefront.

Qualifying Your Suppliers

After you have discovered a handful of companies that you will consider using as your suppliers, you need to begin actually qualifying your suppliers. As a dropshipping store owner, this is the biggest opportunity that you have to ensure that you are working with a supplier who is going to offer the highest quality of products and services possible. Never skip over this step, as doing so could result in you harming your own reputation in a massive way.

Attempt to Communicate with Them

The first thing that you need to do when it comes to qualifying suppliers is attempting to communicate with them. Before you can get anywhere with a supplier, you need to know that you will be able to hold a proper conversation with them so that you can gain access to the information that you need from them. Understand that many dropshipping suppliers are located overseas, which means that some of them are not going to be able to communicate with you as effectively as others. Working together with a dropshipping company that has poor communication, or that struggles to communicate in a timely manner could result in you running into serious issues with your business down the line. You want to look for companies that are able to communicate clearly and effectively and that do so in a timely manner. It should be easy for you to get the information that you need and to ask any questions that you may have, and you should feel confident that the answers that you receive will be complete and easy to understand or act on.

Identify Their Purchasing Process

Next, you want to identify what the purchasing process is with your supplier. You already know that dropshipping means that they will ship directly to your consumer unless you are working with a company like Amazon FBA, in which case they are going to ship directly to your chosen address. That being said, you do want to know about important pieces of information, such as how long it takes for shipping to be fulfilled, what their minimum quantities are, and how they go about fulfilling dropshipping orders. Knowing exactly how they manage their shipping process means that you know what you need to do in order to get the products into the hands of your consumer, which makes your job easier. Never assume that you know what a dropshipping supplier's practices will be, as this can result in you making false assumptions and not getting the quality of service that you expected. In this case, it may not be due to a low-quality supplier but instead due to a miscommunication that results in you looking badly to your consumer.

Ask Them How They Handle Complaints

Before you order anything from a company, you should always ask them how they handle complaints regarding their quality or services. Ensure that you are clear on what their process is for handling returns, how they respond to quality complaints, and what they are going to do if any form of issue arises between you and them or your consumer and them. In dropshipping, you are the go-between, so if something goes wrong between your consumer and your supplier; it will be up to you to resolve the issue and make sure that the consumer is satisfied and that the supplier gets what they need, too. It is important to understand what the processes and procedures are for complaints or returns *before* any problems arise. This way, when they do, you already know how to handle them, and you are able to provide the best quality of service in the most timely manner possible for your consumer. In the end, this will prove to be an important part of making sure that customer complaints do not completely damage your reputation in the long run.

Test the Quality of Products

It is always a good idea to test the quality of products that you want to stock in your business before you ever begin selling them to your audience. Not knowing what the actual quality of the products is can lead to you selling low-quality products without even knowing it. This would be a terrible way to tarnish your reputation in your business, and it can easily be avoided by requesting samples of the products that you are going to be selling in your store.

Many manufacturers and suppliers offer what is called a sample item, which is essentially a special price that you get for ordering just one item, rather than a whole lot of items from their company. This single item represents exactly what you will be selling to your customers and gives you the opportunity to look it over and make sure that it is worthy enough to be sold in your store. Always purchase the sample product and try it out first to make sure that you are selling products that are truly high-quality to your consumers. This is your biggest opportunity to make sure that your customers are getting the best quality of products possible, so do not overlook this step.

Look for Legitimate Reviews

Finally, you need to look for legitimate reviews about the suppliers that you are considering purchasing from, as well as the products that you are considering purchasing from them. Finding reviews on suppliers can be more challenging for the same reason that finding suppliers can be challenging: they do not tend to keep an active presence online. Still, there are some ways that you can find reliable reviews on suppliers before purchasing from them. Searching for reviews is important as it will tell you what to look out for when you shop with a supplier or when you shop for certain products of theirs. Sometimes you might find that your supplier tends to be great to work with and that there is nothing that you need to be cautious about, whereas other times, you might find that there are things that you need to be on the lookout for. Having this information beforehand means that you can feel confident that you know what risks may pose a threat toward your business before you ever get into business with a supplier.

The best way to find honest reviews on companies is to avoid the reviews that they share directly on their websites or pages. If they do have them, these reviews can easily be manipulated by them only choosing to share the highest quality of reviews possible. Even platforms like Amazon, eBay, or Alibaba can have manipulated reviews as suppliers may have their friends purchase low quantities and then leave high-quality reviews, so that the supplier is more likely to make sales to other people.

Instead of looking directly on their pages, you want to go to a platform like Google and search for reviews about suppliers. There will be plenty of peer-based review platforms that come up to help you get real reviews as to whether or not the company is good to work with. Another great way is to find social media groups or online forums where dropshippers come together to support each other in growing their businesses. Groups and forums offer you the opportunity to research the best suppliers and ask questions about potential suppliers, so that you can get real reviews from real-time people. Still, always do your best to make sure that the people who are giving you feedback are real and are not representatives of the supplying company. To do so, simply go to their accounts to see who they are affiliated with and if they have any affiliation with the company that you are seeking to do business with.

Chapter Summary

Choosing strong suppliers for your company gives you the best opportunity to make sure that you are stocking your dropshipping store with products that are sure to earn you money. You always want to make sure that you are choosing the best suppliers possible, so that you can feel confident that you are giving your customers the best products and services possible. Since your suppliers are the ones who will directly serve your customers, it is important that you pick suppliers who are going to represent your company well, so that you do not tarnish your brand name over a low-quality supplier. Although it can be more challenging to find suppliers due to the fact that many do not have a clear or consistent online presence, there are many ways that you can find and qualify suppliers. The increased ease of inability to get started in eCommerce for the average person has led to more companies making their services accessible to average people. This means that there are proven ways to find the best quality of suppliers these days, and these methods are a lot easier than they once were. Always seek to find those high-quality suppliers to ensure that you are getting the best service possible.

Chapter 9: Sales Channels and Marketing Strategies

Getting your product out in front of your audience is an important way for you to grow your dropshipping business. Without the proper sales channels and marketing strategies, you will struggle to get anyone to find your business in the first place so that they can shop with you. These days, most sales channels are saturated, therefore you must combine your sales channels with a strong marketing strategy to ensure that you stand out amongst the rest.

In this chapter, we are going to discuss sales channels that you can use, as well as marketing strategies that are going to help you stand out in those sales channels. This way, you can feel confident that you are reaching your consumers, no matter how many other brands are trying to do the same.

Sales Channels for You to Use

For dropshipping, there are a few different sales channels that you can use. The platforms that we discussed previously often double as sales channels as well and offer you a storefront that you can use to offer your products for sale. However, there are other channels that you can consider using as well. For dropshipping, these channels might include platforms like a hosted storefront, Amazon, Facebook Shops, or Instagram Shops. Each of these sales channels can drive traffic to your products, effectively improving the number of people landing on your sales pages while also decreasing the number of clicks it takes for them to get there.

Each sales channel that you use will require its own unique strategy to ensure that it can effectively bring customers into your business. Below, we will discuss each sales channel and how you can use it to help get your products sold to consumers.

Hosted Storefront

If you choose a base platform that does not host your website, you will need to choose a website to host your storefront on. With your dropshipping business, you need to have a storefront in order for people to have somewhere to purchase your products from, even if you are going to use another platform like Amazon, Facebook, or Instagram. The only exception is if you choose to use Amazon as your platform, as certain Amazon seller plans do offer you to have a separate website and storefront hosted within the Amazon platform.

Your hosted storefront should operate as the main landing hub for all of the marketing strategies that you run within your business. This means that every sales funnel should ultimately lead to your customers landing on your website so that they can purchase your products. If they are not landing on your website, they should be landing on the site where your store is being hosted, such as Amazon, so that they have the opportunity to shop with you. If you run a sales funnel and it is leading people anywhere other than to a checkout page, you are not making the most out of your sales funnel and you are likely going to miss out on many sales due to this very fact.

Amazon

Amazon is by far one of the most powerful dropshipping channels that you can use in the modern age of dropshipping. Aside from Shopify, another powerful platform for dropshipping, Amazon offers virtually everything that you need to generate a strong dropshipping business online. Amazon launched Amazon FBA, or Fulfillment by Amazon, nearly a decade ago now, but it has massively grown in popularity which means that it has also grown to offer far more features for the people who are using it to host their businesses. If you choose to use Amazon FBA, you gain the benefits of a traditional retail eCommerce store and the benefits of dropshipping based on how the service works. With this particular structure, you will purchase products from manufacturers or wholesalers and ship them to an Amazon warehouse so that Amazon employees can then fulfill the dropshipping portion of your business. In other words, you are capable of earning higher profits while still never having to deal directly with the inventory that you are carrying for your business.

If you choose to use Amazon as a sales channel, it is a great idea to take advantage of all of the convenient services that Amazon has to offer, therefore you can really maximize your business. With this platform, you are gaining access to employees who specialize in what they do, including shipping and customer service, making it easier for you to consistently offer the highest quality of services.

Another benefit of using Amazon as a sales channel is that, in addition to granting you access to highly skilled Amazon employees and convenient services, you also gain access to many different marketing channels. With Amazon FBA, you can also use Amazon's paid advertisement features which include banner ads, sponsored products, and advertisements that are hosted elsewhere on the internet such as on blogs and private websites. This means that in addition to organic marketing and native advertisements on social media, you can also get a much wider scale of targeted marketing through Amazon's top of the line marketing structure.

Many dropshippers find that Amazon becomes their secret weapon for success when it comes to generating a strong business with strong sales channels and plenty of opportunities to generate success with their business. With Amazon, you open up an entirely new way of marketing services that you can tap into which makes it an excellent tool for you to use for your dropshipping business.

Social Media Shopping Features

Social media itself is an excellent channel for you to generate sales through. With social media, you can generate interest in sales before people ever even land on your page by advertising what products you have available. This way, when people do land on your website, they already know what they want to buy, and the sale is already made up in their minds, making the purchasing process even easier. This is ultimately the entire goal with sales funnels and marketing, which is why social media is such an incredible tool to use in the first place.

That being said, social media can be taken a step further by using the built-in shopping features on Facebook and Instagram. These shopping features are incredible as they allow you to tag your products in your posts, and then people are able to click those tags and automatically be taken to the product page on your website. This means that if people like what they see, they can shop your posts and purchase your products directly from your website, based on what they have seen on your social media platform.

This particular shopping feature is a key sales funnel strategy as it drives traffic straight to the checkout function on your website. You can create your social media shopping channel by opening a Facebook business page and creating a shoppable page. Then, you simply need to link your Instagram business profile to your Facebook business page and connect your shop features together in the settings function of your profile. From there, you will be able to tag products in your pictures, enabling the entire easy checkout process for your customers. Not only does this make for great sales funnel feature, but it also generates a strong customer experience which makes your brand memorable and enjoyable to shop with.

Building and Operating a Sales Funnel

Sales funnels are the key strategy for any business to get customers through their doors and purchasing their products. Sales funnels have actually existed since businesses first became a thing, but they have evolved drastically over time. Back in the day, a sales funnel primarily consisted of some form of printed advertisement that would also feature information on where to find the physical location for that particular store. Then, all you had to do was go to the store and the sales clerks would walk you through the rest of the funnel by selling their products or services to you.

With eCommerce, sales funnels are still relatively straight forward, but they do require more steps than a single printed advertisement. These days, they require an online presence, a call to action, a website, and a customer experience that keeps them coming back until they purchase from you. In many cases, the sales funnel will continue working to keep them coming back to purchase even more from you. If your sales funnel is effectively reaching people and drawing them through your sales process, then you know that you have successfully built a strong funnel.

The benefit of sales funnels with eCommerce is that the sales funnels are automatic, and so is the sales process. This means that once you have built an effective sales funnel and organized your website accordingly, you can easily draw people through your sales funnel over and over again without ever having to lift a finger. Instead, the automation features that you use on your website can help you get your customers through your sales process.

With eCommerce, the easiest sales funnel to build is one that begins on social media and ends on your website, and then features some form of incentive or reminder to come back. The most basic sales funnel is one where the website has a consistent social media presence that they use to drive people to their website. Then, on their website, people are prompted to sign up for their email newsletter, often in exchange for some form of discount or free bonus that they get just for signing up.

This way, when the customer leaves the website the company can continue to market to them to encourage them to come back to their website and purchase something from them. Often, each email will include some form of a call to action prompting the individual to go to their website, too, to encourage a sale.

Creating a sales funnel like this is easy and does not take much time to create or maintain. You can start by opening up the social media accounts that you will need in order to market to your audience so that you already have these accounts up and running. Once the accounts are open, you want to fill them in with basic information so that they become a "hub" for your business on that particular profile. This means that they should always include your name, contact information, website address, and a basic bio about who you are and what they can expect when doing business with you. As well, you should build up some basic posts so that they have content to see right from the minute that they first land on your page. You will continue uploading posts overtime to ensure that your profile stays relevant and that they see content from you on a regular basis, thereby you stay recent in their memories.

When your profiles have been created, you can use a platform like PLANN or HootSuite to create your posts in advance. These types of platforms let you create and schedule posts out for all of your social media platforms well ahead of time, meaning that you will not actually have to do any work on a day to day basis to keep your platforms updated. Instead, your scheduler will keep the content coming out on a regular basis, and all you need to do is keep your scheduler updated.

Once your profiles are created, you are also going to want to automate any other part of your sales funnel that you choose to use. For example, if you are using an email capture to get the email addresses of people who land on your website so that you can continue to market to them, you will want to automate the welcome emails and the follow-up emails that come out. You can easily create several emails in advance and schedule them out just as you did with your social media posts, in such a way you can continue to have these emails going out even without you needing to fulfill them.

As you create the content for your social media posts and emails, or any other content that you are creating, you need to make sure that you are creating content that directly drives people to your website. This means that everything you write should ultimately encourage people to purchase from your store. The key is to make sure that you are creating content in a way that does not seem spammy or like your only purpose is to get people on your website. Instead, you want to use your brand personality to create content that is relatable, interesting, and conversational, and use that to drive people to your website. By doing so, people are interested in what you have to say and are more likely to follow through with your call to action, rather than them seeing that your only purpose is to drive them to your website resulting in them losing interest.

The last part of your business that you can automate is sponsored posts and paid advertisements. Platforms like Amazon, Google, Facebook, Instagram, and other social media platforms all offer paid advertisement features that you can use to drive traffic to your website without having to rely so much on organic marketing features. Creating strong advertisements and then investing an advertising budget into them every month can help you reach people beyond your basic organic market, so that you can drive even more traffic to your page. Plus, if you create and schedule them effectively, your paid advertisements can continue to work on an automated basis alongside the rest of your sales funnel.

Once everything is automated, all you need to do is continue to create automated content for your sales funnel. Aside from creating new content to be automated and posted on a consistent basis, you should not have to do anything else to maintain your sales funnel.

Analyzing Your Analytics

As you are automating your content for your sales funnel, it is important that you pause to track the analytics for your previous content. At first, this will not be possible because you will not have any historical analytics for you to pay attention to. In this case, only automate a week or so at a time so that you can begin to build up analytics for your business. Then, once you have, you can begin tracking your analytics to show you how your content is performing with your audience.

In business, your analytics can tell you exactly what you need to post more of, in order to get in front of your audience and stay in front of them. Following your analytics closely can tell you what your audience finds to be relevant, what topics they are interested in learning about, and what trends they are following. All of this information can support you with getting your content in front of your audience and building your reputation, making it well worth the effort.

You can find analytics regarding your past marketing strategies in the platforms that you have been marketing on. All business pages on social media profiles have built-in analytics features, and so do most automated email service providers and platforms like Amazon, Shopify, Squarespace, or any other platform that you may choose to use to host your actual sales through.

Chapter Summary

Creating sales channels and marketing strategies for your business is a crucial way for you to get your business in front of customers. Your sales channels are windows of opportunity for your customers to see what products you have available and how they can purchase them from you. It also gives your customers the opportunity to identify what your brand is and develop brand recognition and brand loyalty, as they continue to interact with your marketing outreach strategies such as your social media presence.

When it comes to creating a strong sales channel and sales funnels, you need to identify exactly how your customers will land on your website and then nurture these strategies. Using automation tools is a great opportunity for you to ensure that your business can continue running, and your sales funnels can continue functioning even without you getting involved in actually sharing content on a day to day basis.

The best way to make sure that your automation features continue to work and that you continue to drive traffic through your sales funnel is to schedule a day every week, every second week, or every month for you to automate your marketing materials. Refrain from automating too far in advance as this can make adjusting your approach to suit your analytic findings and trend findings challenging. Each time you upload new automated content, make sure that you are tracking your analytics to upload content that is capable of helping you grow your business effectively. This way, you can feel confident that all of the content you are uploading is relevant to your audience.

Chapter 10: All about Orders

Orders with dropshipping happen differently from traditional eCommerce orders because the retailer selling the products has nothing to do with the products themselves. Despite this fact, it is still important that you understand the order process and the role you play in it to know how you can contribute to successful ordering experiences for your customers. This will also help you know what to do should any troubles arise, so that you are taking all of the necessary actions to offset these risks and develop your business.

In this chapter, we will discuss everything about orders, ranging from how to deal with them and what to do should any troubles arise during the ordering process.

Security

Creating a secure purchasing experience for your customers is crucial for them, as well as for you. In this day and age, people will rarely purchase online unless they feel confident that their purchases will be safe and that they are not investing their money into a scam. Improving security with your business by creating a secure checkout process for your customers is vital. The best way that you can improve order security is by using a strong platform like Amazon, Shopify, BigCommerce, WooCommerce, or any other well-known platform that can offer a strong checkout process. Refrain from using any unknown platform or one that seems to lack strong ratings, as this could result in your checkout process not being nearly as secure. Stick to well-known names so that your customers feel confident and safe when purchasing with you.

Fraud Issues

Using a well-known point of sale platform is a great way to eliminate fraud issues within your business. Ideally, you want to use a platform that will protect both yourself and your customers from possible fraud so that everyone feels safe as they use the checkout process. One big type of fraud that dropshippers face is credit card fraud, where people will purchase products through them with a credit card and then order a chargeback through their credit card company to receive the funds back. This results in them having to pay for the product that the individual received, and the individual receiving a refund for that product. In other words, they end up getting the product for free, and in many cases, they will go on to sell the product so that they can earn the profit from it instead.

Protecting your company from credit card fraud starts with using a company like Amazon or Shopify which has built-in features that are meant to protect merchants like you against this type of fraud. In these cases, certain shipping labels are used, which prove that the product was delivered, making it more challenging for the individual to request a chargeback.

Another thing you can do to look out for possible cases of fraud is to check for common red flags that indicate that fraud could be taking place. For credit card fraud, the common signs include an individual who has different billing and shipping addresses, different names, strange emails that appear to be fake, rush shipping, especially on expensive purchases, package re-routing, or unusually large orders. All of these behaviors are common behaviors that take place when credit card fraud is happening and can massively impact your business. If you notice any suspicious behaviors like this taking place, you can take action to prevent the sale from going through with your company.

One great way that you can minimize fraud and prevent chargebacks is by using a managed services solution, which is a company that pays attention to your incoming orders to prevent the risk of fraud. As your company grows, this may be an ideal opportunity for you to avoid being put at risk of these forms of fraud. A great company to consider should you want to use a service like this is ClearSale, which has built-in features that monitor your orders and flag possible fraudulent orders to prevent them from going through.

Product Returns

A strict return policy can prevent you from having to deal with returns or refunds, but it can also drive people away from doing business with you since they cannot effectively test out your products to guarantee that they like them. If your return and refund policy is too strict, customers may not want to purchase from you because they will worry that if they have a problem, they cannot receive any support with the problem they have faced. Instead, they will go elsewhere to another business that has a better return or refund policy to purchase the same products.

Managing product returns and refunds with dropshipping can get messy, especially because the product has already been purchased from the wholesaler, which makes it more challenging for you to manage it. With dropshipping, you are dealing with the wholesaler's return policy, which means that if they have a strict return policy, you may have to refund the product and take it into your own possession, which begs the question: what then?

The best way to create strong return policies for your business is to choose suppliers who also have decent return policies, so that you can return the product directly to the supplier. Alternatively, you can use a company like Amazon FBA who completely manages all returns and refunds for you, and resells returned products to future customers. This way, rather than having returned products sitting in your own possession and with no way of really selling them, other than by selling them privately, they are all dealt with properly.

Shipping Issues

Running into shipping issues when you are a dropshipper can be challenging. Some suppliers take days or even weeks to work through these problems, which can make it even more challenging for you to deal with them. If you, as a merchant, take too long to deal with shipping issues, it can become a huge problem for your business. The best way to deal with shipping issues is to pick a carrier and then use that same carrier for every single shipment. For example, you could use the U.S. Postal Service or a shipping company like UPS or FedEx to do all of your shipping through. These services offer small businesses tools that they can use to calculate shipping on products, making it easier for those small businesses to offer consistent shipping rates. Alternatively, you could use Amazon FBA, which has its own shipping service that tends to be cheaper than going through your own private shipping deal with a company.

International Shipments

International shipments can be dealt with in the same way as domestic ones are, however, the pricing will be different. Offering a separate shipping option that provides prices for international customers is ideal to ensure that they are being charged for the entire shipping fee. This also ensures that you are not charging too much for the shipping fee, which could drive international customers away. Ideally, you should use the same carrier for international shipping that you use for domestic shipping, such that your shipping concerns are always easy for you to navigate.

Dealing with Out of Stock Orders

Most of the suppliers you work with will be supplying multiple dropshipping companies just like yours. This means that accidents can happen where the products they have to go out of stock and, on your website, it shows up as if they are still in stock. Unless you are using a company duo like Oberlo and Shopify, real-time updates are not often available, which implies that you could run into issues around this.

If a customer does order an out-of-stock product, the next best thing you can do is communicate with your supplier to determine when the product will be back in stock. If they are in stock quickly, you may be able to just let things go on as usual. Otherwise, it may be ideal to message that customer, offer an apology, and refund that part of their order. You may also consider offering them some form of an added bonus to make up for the inconvenience, such as free shipping on the rest of their order or a discount for their next purchase. In many cases, simply letting them know and offering a solution such as one of the ones previously mentioned will help you navigate these issues relatively seamlessly.

Inventory

While you run your dropshipping company, it is ideal to make sure that you have a system to help you identify how much stock is left in any given product, so that you can feel confident that you have plenty for your customers to order. If you use a simple company like Amazon FBA, this will be easy as Amazon updates your numbers on your dashboard to let you know how much stock you have left. Otherwise, you will have to regularly check in with your suppliers to see how inventory levels are going, in order that you know that there is plenty left for your customers to order. If you find that inventory levels with your supplier are low, you can always set a product to "out of stock" even before it officially goes out of stock to avoid running into this problem.

Chapter Summary

Dealing with orders in a dropshipping business can be somewhat tricky as you are more of a middle man than an actual retailer. Knowing how to manage orders and how to prevent fraudulent purchases or other troubles from taking place during the ordering process is important as this helps you prevent any issues from arising in your business. It is important that you educate yourself on all protocols around your orders with every single supplier you use to know exactly what you need to do in the event of any form of order trouble. This way, everything can always be dealt with in a timely manner and without causing too significant troubles for you or anyone else involved in the ordering and order fulfillment process.

Chapter 11: How to Expand Your Dropshipping Business

Over time, you will want to expand your dropshipping business so that you can begin to earn even more money through your company. Their process of expanding your business is simple, especially if you already begin to generate success with the early steps that you have taken to grow your business. In this chapter, we will discuss the most effective process for you to grow your dropshipping business to continue to generate greater levels of success as you go.

Creating A "Rinse and Repeat" Approach

The easiest way for you to grow your dropshipping business is to create a "rinse and repeat" approach that allows you to do the same thing over and over while growing your results along the way. When you are creating a rinse and repeat approach, your goal is to outline the basic steps you needed to take to reach success with your business. For example, maybe you start by listening to your audience, generating a message that spoke directly to them, and then identifying products that you could share through that message in order to earn sales. You may also have an outlined strategy for how you chose those products, how you marketed them, and how you got them in front of the eyes of new possible customers, thus you could earn greater sales in your business.

Rather than attempting to recreate your entire approach, you can repeat these steps over and over again, with the intention of building on your momentum and reaching even more customers than you did previously. As you repeat your process time and again, make sure to note down what has worked and what hasn't, as this will allow you to refine your approach. As a result, you will be able to continue reaching your audience in a larger way every time, effectively growing your business out in a stronger and more effective manner.

In the issue of growing your business, the biggest strategy that you can invest in is momentum. Every time you make a sale, use that to generate momentum to create even more sales, as this will ultimately help your business grow and will support you with reaching more people. You generate momentum every time you celebrate new products going out, rave about the reviews you are receiving, and promote the fact that multiple people are experiencing great success with your products so far. You can easily incorporate these facts into your automated marketing strategy to further promote your products and boost your brand credibility, while also building out your momentum.

Reinvesting into Your Own Business

As you continue to grow your business, it is a good idea to plan to continually reinvest your profits into your growing business. This does not mean that you should not keep any profits from yourself, but you should be reinvesting a fair amount back into your business. This reinvested capital can be used to pay for targeted advertisement campaigns, to add higher quality features to your automation strategy or website, or to otherwise invest in features that are either going to improve your outreach or improve your customer experience.

Chapter Summary

Scaling a business has more to do with building momentum than it does with anything else. When it comes to scaling your dropshipping business, you need to be ready to continually improve on your rinse and repeat strategy to help you grow. This way, you can continue to build on the momentum that you have already begun to create so that you can grow your business out even further. As you do, make sure that you reinvest your capital into your business to pay for better features and services and pay for a greater reach with your paid advertising. This way, you can improve your customer experience while also reaching a larger audience, effectively helping you grow your business and give your customers many more reasons to come purchase with you going forward.

Chapter 12: How to Avoid Beginner's Mistakes

When it comes to dropshipping, there are many mistakes that you need to be aware of as a beginner so that you can avoid making these mistakes and stunting your success early on. Being aware of these mistakes in advance can help you bypass them, therefore you can get a better head start in reaching the level of success that you desire to reach with your business. Using this head start is a great way to give yourself a competitive edge and reach a greater level of success than your peers are in less timing, too.

Worrying About Shipping Costs

One big mistake that you need to avoid as a beginner is worrying about shipping costs. Many new dropshippers will calculate and recalculate their shipping costs over and over again before ever making a sale, all to make sure that they have charged the right amount. The truth is, there are other things that you need to worry about more than shipping costs. Instead, set your shipping costs and then focus on getting sales into your business. You can always adjust your shipping costs in the future if you find that you have made a mistake at any point.

Excessive Reliance on Vendors

In the issue of running a dropshipping business, your vendors are crucial for getting products into the hands of your customers. Because of that, you should never make the mistake of placing excessive reliance on any single vendor, as this could result in you having serious issues going forward. Instead, have a few vendors that you can get your products from so that if anything goes wrong with one vendor, such as products going out of stock, you have another vendor you can go to for support.

Not Creating a Strong Customer Experience

When it comes to any business, your customer experience is a crucial step in helping you get your customers to your website to actually purchase from you. Many dropshippers forget that even though dropshipping is plug-in-and-go from the back end, it still requires a strong customer experience on the front end. You need to build a strong brand and incorporate that into a strong customer experience if you generate any level of success with your business.

Mishandling Order Issues

I placed a heavy emphasis on the importance of understanding order protocol for a reason: it helps to have access to this information right from the start so that should any issues arise, you know what you need to do to help your customer. The less information you have to retrieve in the event of trouble, the quicker you can manage these problems. This means that if anything goes wrong, you are likely going to be able to handle it in the best way possible and in minimal timing so that you do not completely destroy your reputation over it. Nothing will sink you faster than mishandling order issues like refunds, returns, or shipping-related issues.

Not Creating a Return Feature

As an attempt to avoid issues relating to refunds or returns, many dropshipping companies create a strict no returns and no refunds policy that is meant to avoid them from having to deal with them altogether. Although this may seem as though it will make your job a lot easier, it will also drive away your customers as they will fear that you will not help them should they have an issue with their order. Instead, you should go through the effort of creating a strong return and refund policy that offers assistance to your customers if they are not satisfied, without causing excessive issues for yourself. Knowing your order protocol will help you determine a refund and return policy that fits your business and offers a reasonable solution for dissatisfied customers.

Chapter 13: Additional Tips

Generating strong success as a business comes from more than just sidestepping possible mistakes and following the plan to a point. You also need to know what you can do to improve your chances at success by knowing what to look out for and how you can best support your business with growth. In life and business, one of the best ways to gain access to this additional information is through hands-on experience, which helps you collect your own information for your business. That being said, much of this information can also be shared with you from others who have already been there, such as myself! In this chapter, we will discuss five important tips that you can use to help you build a strong dropshipping business that will turn you a great profit month over month.

Have a Backup Plan

You should always have a backup plan for everything in your business. This goes for everything from which you are getting your supplies from to which web host you are using, and which shipping company you are going through. You should always have a clear backup plan for what you will do if any step in your process goes wrong. You can also have a backup plan for your backup plan so that you are truly prepared in any given scenario that you may face. Having backup plans ensures that your business continues to run smoothly, no matter what circumstances you may face, which is important to prevent you from losing your momentum or disrupting your reputation due to a possible setback.

Invest in Your Marketing Skills

Your key role in your dropshipping business is marketing, as you will need to market your sales funnel to get people through it, so that they purchase from you. Investing in your marketing skills by attending seminars, reading up on the latest marketing trends, and paying attention to your competition to see how you can improve your own skills is important. The better you are at marketing, the more people you will get through your sales funnel, which will result in even more people purchasing from your business.

Automate Your Business Wherever Possible

One of the best things about a dropshipping company is that it can be automated, allowing you to turn it into a highly passive stream of income. Whenever you can, always automate your business in order to continue to run seamlessly, regardless of where you are at or what is going on in your life. Automating your business not only allows you to let it run itself when you are away, but it also allows you to feel confident that every piece of marketing material fits together well and contributes to your greater image in the best way possible.

Create a High-quality Website

Your website says a lot about your brand, which is why you should invest in a high-quality website. Being cheap on your website may sound like a good way to save money early on, but it can also drastically impact your reputation in the long run. Instead, spend as much as you can afford on a high-quality website that looks great and offers a high-quality customer experience. You can always invest in other things, such as paid marketing, later on. This way, your customers get a high-quality experience right from the start, and you never build the reputation of having a business website that is hard to purchase from or difficult to navigate.

Be Ready to Pivot When Needed

Any good business needs to be ready to adjust their approach as needed, and the same goes for you. If you want to have a strong dropshipping business, you need to be ready to pivot your approach at any given moment to a new direction that is going to help serve your growth. Stay focused on your analytics and pay attention to market trends to make sure that you are always growing in the most profitable direction, and do not be afraid to take a full pivot as needed, so that you can stay where the profits are.

Chapter 14: Case History from Successful Dropshippers

Although the strategy of dropshipping itself has been used since as early as the 50s when multi-level marketing and network marketing became a thing, the term dropshipping is rather new. In around 2006, dropshipping launched alongside the introduction of Amazon's FBA feature. Since then, a massive and growing list of people has turned dropshipping into a successful venture for themselves and has generated massive amounts of success over the years.

One of the most impressive dropshipping success stories belongs to a man named Irwin Dominguez, who made $1 million in profits in just 8 months of dropshipping. Dominguez launched his company alongside a friend who was generating decent success in his business and found that he, too, managed to turn a huge profit in minimal timing. He created his success by learning about eCommerce through Google, launching a Shopify account, and stocking that Shopify store with

Oberlo. On his best days, Dominguez earns about $30,000 per day, but he averages around $10,000 per day. Dominguez recommends validating your product and starting small before moving into large quantities of products and shipments, to ensure that you know your industry well before leaping into the deep end. This way, you are prepared for the amount of work it will take to sustain a larger dropshipping company. He also suggests that you prepare for the amount of work that the successful days will take, as you may have to do more on those days to help keep your shop stocked and support customers with any concerns they may have within your business.

Kate is another great story of dropshipping success, as she earned $32,000+ per month through her business. Kate started out with Aliexpress in their eCommerce department, and she creates and tests our promotion strategies for dropshipping stores, so that she can support them with their growth. Just three years ago, Kate knew nothing about dropshipping, and now she is earning a massive profit every single month from the strategies that she has created and tested. Kate recommends growing into offering a large variety of products and using platforms like Instagram to get your products out there. She also suggests using a simple rinse and repeat approach that she calls "duplicate and modify," whereby you can build on your momentum and get your business even further out there, helping you expand and increase your sales every single month.

A power couple that exists in the dropshipping world is Aloysius Chay and Galvin Bay. This partnership earns $60,000 per day after just a year of starting their dropshipping store. These two suggests that you always learn about new products and offer those products in your shop, whereby you are continually offering products that people actually want to buy. The more that you can keep your shop up to date and offer products that people want, the more reason they have to purchase with you and order products through your website. They also recommend staying on your toes so that you are always ready to offer the latest and greatest, or deal with any issues or challenges that may arise as your business is growing. According to these two, any business that is not growing is slowly dying, so you should always be on the lookout for ways to grow.

These are just three of the countless success stories out there regarding the dropshipping industry. If you want to become one of those success stories, the strategies outlined in this very book will take you there. Use them to cultivate your foundation and then build your own rinse and repeat approach in order to evolve your business and grow even more successful each week. This way, you truly can make a massive success out of your dropshipping business.

Conclusion

Dropshipping has been around for nearly two decades, yet it still proves to be a highly effective business model for turning a profit online. These days, if you want to be a dropshipper there is plenty of information out there about how you can get started and what you need to do in order to turn your business into a success. The key for you is to ensure that the information you are reading is relevant and high-quality so that you can find yourself amongst the top earners in this industry.

I hope that through reading *Dropshipping for Beginners,* you were able to identify a strong approach for you to get into dropshipping and earn a profit. By giving you some insight as to what this industry is and a clear strategy for how you can get started and grow your business, I hope that you now feel confident in generating your own success. If you really want to make the most out of this information, you need to be ready to apply it with consistency and confidence every step of the way so that you can generate a huge income through your business.

The next step after reading this book is to research what industries are the most successful for dropshipping and then find yourself a niche that you can build in. After that, you can begin to create your brand and grow your business through developing an online presence for you to reach your customers with.

Make sure that you start small and grow out, as this is the best way to ensure that you test your niche first so that you can validate its profitability. If your results are promising, you can use this information to help you increase your sales and grow your business out even further. As well, don't forget to check out my other titles like *Amazon FBA* so that you can further grow your knowledge in this industry! Knowing exactly what you can do to grow your business through strong sales channels will help you get your name out there and maximize your success in this industry.

You also need to make sure that you pay close attention to the tips and advice that I have given you, as this information can help you succeed even faster. The information I have provided you with here is intended to help you quickly grow beyond many beginners' mistakes and challenges, whereby you can step into mastering your dropshipping business right from day one. Avoid underestimating this advice, as it truly can help set you apart and guarantee your success in the industry!

If you enjoyed this book, I invite you to rate it on Amazon Kindle. Your honest feedback about *Dropshipping for Beginners* would be great, as this helps me create more high-quality guides for people just like you!

Lastly, I recommend reading my other two books _Amazon FBA_ and _Online Marketing Strategies 2020,_ so that you can widen the overall vision of the online business world.

Thank you, and best of luck in your dropshipping business!

Made in the USA
Las Vegas, NV
25 November 2024